GREEN CATHEDRALS

BRIAN ALEXANDER

CATHEDRALS

LYONS & BURFORD, PUBLISHERS L&B

FOR MOM AND DAD,
WHO KEPT TELLING ME TO GO OUTSIDE AND PLAY.

PRINTED IN THE UNITED STATES OF AMERICA
DESIGN BY KATHY KIKKERT
10 9 8 7 6 5 4 3 2 1

LIBRARY OF CONGRESS CATALOGING-IN-PUBLICATION DATA

ALEXANDER, BRIAN, 1959–
    GREEN CATHEDRALS / BRIAN ALEXANDER.
        P. CM.
    ISBN 1-55821-399-6 (CLOTH)
    1. RAIN FORESTS—ANECDOTES. 2. ALEXANDER, BRIAN,
1959—JOURNEYS. I. TITLE.
QH86.A58 1995
304.2—DC20   95–23739
                            CIP

CONTENTS

ACKNOWLEDGMENTS

I have been lucky to meet some very helpful people along the way, without whom this book would not have been possible. Many are mentioned in these pages and their contributions are obvious. I would also like to give special thanks to the following people, in no particular order: Shelley Metcalf; Winifred Golden; Ata Rivers; Michael Goulding; Nanette Wiser; Julia Craig; Sue Brush; Wendy Lothspeich; Elizabeth Vasey; Arthur Demarest; Jane Rai; Deanne Yamamoto; the crew at Alaska Discovery; Wildlife Conservation International; Conservation International; the staff of *Outside* magazine, especially Alex Heard and Kathy Martin; Copley News Service; John Benditt at *Science*; Arthur Salm, who first suggested a book; my friends at the *Toronto Sun*; Lisa Gabor for her support and advice; Francesca Hayslett, who applied her sharp eye to the unenviable task of critiquing a friend's work; Amy Young for supporting the project; Peter Burford for making the book better than it would have been; and Gail Chaffee, who gave lots and got little.

CROSSROADS
(MALAYSIA)

They threatened to kill me if I carried drugs into Malaysia. There was a sign saying so at the baggage carousel, a greeting that sure beat "Welcome to Malaysia" as an eye-catcher. Not that I was carrying anything stronger than Kaopectate and vitamins, but visions of *Midnight Express* ran through my head and I wondered for a moment if, in fact, somebody had not managed to sneak a couple of kilos into my bag or if my white vitamin C tablets could possibly be mistaken for contraband. But a sign like that was uniquely Malaysian. It said "please." It was sincere. It was humble. It was reassuring to know Malaysia was a country where they warned you nicely before they killed you.

As I stumbled into a cab for the drive into Kuala Lumpur, I asked the driver for my hotel. He smiled, gave me a funny, questioning look, shifted the car into drive and began to search for topics of conversation. How about that Kuala Lumpur soccer team? he asked in his Hindi accent. I could have been in New York. But along the way he mentioned something about an arch, a sultan, and Islam. That was a tour I had never had in New York. Too bad it was pitch dark outside. Too bad I was barely conscious after something like a day in an airplane that travelled through a handful of time zones and a dateline.

With a black canvas to imagine on, and with exhaustion inducing hallucinations, my imagination ran a little wild. Sultans. Mosques. Asia. And rain forest jungles out of Conrad.

Which is exactly what I had hoped. I had come to write a story on Taman Negara, the country's rain-forest national park reputed to be the oldest tropical rain forest on the planet. The park was supposed to be home to the Sumatran rhino, the smallest rhinocerous species and one of the twelve most endangered animals in the world. Estimates of how many rhinos lived in Taman Negara varied but there were thought to be under twenty.

The Sumatran rhino, like all rhino species, was victim to a kind of perverse blood libel prevalant throughout Asia that the use of its ground horn could make a man more sexually potent. Of course the rhino did not sit still for the removal of its horn and had to be killed, a high price to pay so a guy in Tokyo could have an erection. I wanted to see one of these rhinos in the wild, to meet the people still living in the jungle, to enter my own little Heart of Darkness. I was pretty sure it would all happen.

But this was Malaysia. My driver snapped me out of my exotic reverie when we pulled up to the hotel. "Here we are, Mr. Mak Gyver," he said.

"Sorry?" I said, thinking his thick accent had slaughtered Mac, as in "Hey, Mac, you owe me ten bucks."

He smiled broadly, a look that said, I know you, you can't fool me. "You are Mr. Mak Gyver, the famous American television star."

"Mak Gyver?" I asked. "Oh, McGyver, the secret agent. No, I'm not McGyver."

He was crestfallen. I apologized for not being McGyver and walked into the lobby of the hotel past a young, pretty Asian woman in a red dress that was far too short and much too back-less to be in an Islamic country where they threaten to kill you at the airport. She was with a western businessman. They were coming out of the lobby bar. He was smiling that stupid grin men get when they are feeling a little sheepish and are about to part with money. They pushed the elevator call button and entered the car, giggling.

I was confused. Maybe this WAS New York. Maybe I was already asleep. I checked in, rode the elevator up, cracked open my door, and dumped my bag on the floor. The room clock read 11:30. My body clock had stopped.

When I threw the curtains open the following morning, I did not see New York. I saw Dallas. I turned on the radio and heard stock quotes from the Dow Jones. I went downstairs for breakfast. In the lobby, western, Chinese, and Malay businessmen had brief-cases tucked under their arms. Dallas with an accent. But then I walked across the street from my very modern hotel to a small café where I hoped to get some breakfast. The special of the day was fresh frog congee. And even in Dallas the Baptists don't stop tele-vision programming for the recitation of prayers the way the Mus-lims do in Kuala Lumpur and the rest of Malaysia. I imagined the uproar as the picture suddenly turned to a Baptist preacher read-ing from the Bible just as the Cowboys were driving down the field.

The car pulled onto a narrow road at the back end of the town of Kuala Tembeling after a four-hour drive northeast from Kuala Lumpur. I got out, thanked my driver, and looked to the bank of a muddy river at a small dock lined with dugout canoes. The canoes had enormous outboards clamped onto their sterns. A crowd of young men, mostly teenagers, hung out on the dock smoking and working on engines. A shack on the dock was decorated with a calendar. A girl in a bikini stroked a black 75-horsepower Mercury.

I sat on the grass overlooking the river waiting to board the boat that would take me into the jungle.

An Australian family, half a dozen Japanese schoolboys singing songs, and a few German couples joined me on the riverbank. A young German and his new bride were clearly off to a bad start. This was their honeymoon. She stared at the dense green on the other side of the river, her T-shirt already damp with sweat extruded by the tropical heat, apparently with thoughts of Ibiza or Nice and cocktails on a beach floating in her head. He swatted a mosquito and looked sideways at her, perhaps realizing he'd pay for this choice of a honeymoon getaway for the rest of his life.

Half an hour later one of the teenage boys walked up the bank and announced "Taman Negara," the signal to climb aboard one of the canoes, the only way to get to the interior. The boy who made the announcement sat by his engine, flicked his cigarette butt into the Tembeling River, and threw on the gas.

The ride upriver to Kuala Tahan, the gateway to Taman Negara, was supposed to take about three hours. That was a very rough figure. The Tembeling, part of the Pahang River system, the largest in Malaysia, originated in the mountainous spine of the peninsula and was fed by rain runoff. It careened wildly from tame in summer to out of control during the winter monsoons. In January, the water level could be thirty feet higher in spots than in August. Then, upstream travel slowed to a crawl.

But this was late August, the river was tame, and the sky was blue. A few minutes out, the boat began to pass small riverside villages. Semi-tame water buffalo lounged along the banks or lulled on sandbars half submerged in the cool water. Elderly village men dressed in sarongs stood by rickety wooden steps leading from their shacks to the water's edge, where they dropped their sarongs to bathe. They all gave friendly waves to the passing boat.

There were also a few other boats on the river. As it had for thousands of years, the Tembeling served as the main transportation route into and out of the region. Most villagers could never afford the price of a car, and even if they could, there was no road from Kuala Tahan to the west. The road to the east was dirt, or, in winter, mud.

About an hour into the trip, we passed a ramshackle conglomeration of thatch-covered lean-tos sitting on a sandbar. About twenty people were wandering among the structures. Women held small naked black children in their arms. Men in loincloths and old T-shirts waded in the river. No one waved.

I looked back at the boat's skipper, who sat squatting next to the engine with his hand on the throttle. He saw the question in my eyes.

"Orang Asli," he said a little dismissively.

He couldn't be bothered with a tour. The pilot taking this diverse group of tourists upriver was a true boat jockey, a river teamster. He was one of an unofficial guild of boatmen who ran the water when it was high and snaked around—and sometimes over—gravel beds when it was low. When they were not ferrying passengers on their boats, they were tearing them apart like some testosterone-pumped American kid with his head under the roof of a Mustang.

We reached Kuala Tahan, a village of about 250 people, two hours after leaving the Tembeling dock, good speed for the boatmen. I looked around for a man a friend in Kuala Lumpur had suggested I meet, a man named Halim, who, my friend said, I would find very interesting. Within a few seconds of our landing, a waiflike fellow jogged up to me and introduced himself as Halim. There was plenty of daylight left, he said, so why not look around?

As we climbed the steep bank leading into the village, the trees began to disappear. The forest was gone. A few months before, it had been cut down. The government was establishing another rubber plantation. The residents greeted the destruction of the forest as good news. A new plantation would mean jobs as tappers and other workers. The dirt road would be improved.

I asked Halim how he felt about the cutting of the forest.

"People need to eat. We are lucky we have the national park, but people cannot live off the national park. This is going to happen all over." For Halim it was fate.

"The government is selling the forest," said Abdul Mutalib bin Jamaludin. Abdul Mutalib, son-in-law of the village chief, operated a tiny hostel in Kuala Tahan. He used to be a teacher, but now made about twice as much money putting up eco-tourists, mainly Malaysians. He employed three people. Still, he did not see the cutting of the forest as a problem.

"Here the villagers need some development also, so we need to cut the forest. At least we are replacing trees with trees." He also saw the rubber plantation as another tourist attraction. People could watch the latex drip out of the trunks.

Perhaps, Halim chimed in, the money earned from the rubber plantation could finance a research institute to study Taman Negara and educate people about Asian rain forests. Well, maybe. But a more immediate concern was what the sultan of Pahang would do with his acreage. To get the sultan's assent to the sale of so much land in his realm, the government had to buy him off, a standard practice in such cases. This time, the government gave him five thousand adjacent hectares. He was free to do as he pleased with the land. If the past was any indication, the sultan would go for the quick money, sell timber rights, and head for Pebble Beach.

Nobody told the officials in charge of the park that the sale was under way. A ranger, trained in the U.S., was livid. "Taman Negara doesn't even know what it has," he said a few days later. He had wanted a buffer zone around the park, something he knew he would never get. "There is not very good coordination here at all," he complained.

Taman Negara meant, simply, National Park. It was one of the largest preserves of tropical rain forest in Asia. The park had its genesis as a much smaller game preserve in 1925. The idea of roping it off was first proposed by English birders and amateur naturalists. In 1938–39 the colonial government grabbed 4,343 square kilometers of land from the three sultans of Kelantan, Pahang, and Trengganu and dubbed the area, naturally, King George V National Park. After independence, Malaysia, naturally, changed the name to Taman Negara.

If Taman Negara had not been set aside when it was, it never would have been. It was preserved on the cusp of World War II. Then Britain was asked, politely, of course, since that's the way Malaysians do everything, to go home. There would be no setting aside such a large piece of land ever again. In fact, in its rush for development, Malaysia almost flooded most of Taman Negara by damming a river. The land was surveyed, the brass and concrete markers driven into the soil, and the bulldozers positioned. Only the end of the Middle East oil crisis, an event that made the dam uneconomical, prevented the loss of the park. But another dam was later built, this one on the Pergau River north of Taman Negara. This dam, largely financed by the British government in return for a Malaysian promise to buy £1.3 billion worth of British arms, embarrassed then-foreign secretary Douglas Hurd when a British court ruled the tit-for-tat deal illegal.

Politics, arms, development, forests, Islam, the past, the future. They all seemed to be converging on Taman Negara like a small town at a crossroads. So much for Conrad and my Heart of Darkness. And nobody had even mentioned rhinos. I did not think much of my prospects for finding any answers to my questions. It was all getting to be thick stew and I did not have a spoon.

Halim did, and, frighteningly, he seemed to make as much sense as anybody. Halim had an opinion on everything, and it was usually bizarre. He knew, for example, that the CIA was actually behind the cholesterol scare sweeping the western world. Cholesterol, he claimed, was a plot to discredit palm oil, a substance loaded with the artery-clogging stuff and one of Malaysia's leading exports. The CIA wanted to break Malaysia. And by the way, the CIA was also responsible for other problems that he was not at liberty to discuss.

A jungle man of the inscrutable east, Halim, rail thin and slightly built, would turn out to be a puzzle. He was about as close to Jesus as you could get in Muslim Malaysia. He owned a couple of T-shirts, a pair of rubber sandals, a pair of shorts, a pair of trousers, a pair of nylon sweatpants, and a rucksack. He stayed in the forest for months on end living on rice and plants, and when he emerged, his head filled with new ideas he had concocted, friends in Kuala Tahan put him up. A lodge across the river from the village fed him.

He read whatever he could scrounge and soaked up the words like a sponge. During our time together he quoted *The Economist*, the Bible, the Koran, *USA Today*, Ghandi, Sufi mystics, the Asian *Wall Street Journal*, and the *Toronto Globe and Mail*. Halim was nothing if not curious. Somehow he had mixed everything together and arrived at his own philosophy of "natural law," a philosophy that changed daily and depended largely on the issue he happened to be discussing. But after I'd spent several days with Halim, it all began to make a strange sort of sense.

While Halim might have been regarded as a street-corner crank in North America, or even in a modern city like Kuala Lumpur, the locals and the Orang Asli, whose language Halim had picked up during his time in the jungle, thought him privy to some heavy wisdom. Halim had some influence in Kuala Tahan and the scattered villages up and down the river, influence based at least partly on a perception of his mysterious weirdness. This did not sit well with the local Muslim leadership. Halim was raised Muslim. And Islamic fundamentalists were gaining power in the north of Malaysia, a region that began roughly in the area of Taman Negara. Halim's ideas were hardly orthodox, and the clerics insisted it just would not do to have a Muslim running around the jungle expounding a self-invented "natural law." Halim's philosophy made him worry about the loss of the jungle. Malaysians were not supposed to be worried about the loss of the jungle, nor about the loss of primitive culture. Malaysia was sprinting headlong into the future, after all, and was actively trying to lose primitive culture. Most Malaysians figured the jungle was a place for normal people to avoid. To the villagers it was some place to get away from, not hike into. Many were only a generation or two removed from it and they liked the outside world better. They had discovered Michael Jordan, Winstons in a hard pack, and Coke, all developments Halim thought were disturbing. There was, for example, the case of *Nightmare on Elm Street IV*.

Somehow, a pirated copy of the video cassette had found its way up the Tembeling and into Kuala Tahan where a few people owned VCRs powered by generators. The tape had played in every VCR in the village to boffo box office. Then it travelled to smaller villages and back again to Kuala Tahan. This had been going on for months. Most people in the villages had seen Freddy Kreuger slash throats a few dozen times. Halim disapproved.

"It makes them want everything modern," he said. "These are bad influences on the people." And yet Halim favored the rubber plantation; he favored development. He did not see the contradiction. But the villagers wanted more of the First World. They wanted a new road, and cars, and jeans and movies. The cat was out of the bag.

One day Halim and I took a boat upriver about twenty kilometers. We hiked into the jungle. After we had been walking for about an hour, he casually said "You know, Halim is not my real name. Nobody knows my real name. It is important that some people do not know where I am. It is because of the brainwashing experiments to make me violent." I smiled and scanned the trail for a sharp stick.

It was during the race riots, he explained.

Malaysia is made up of three distinct races. The Malays, a people anthropologists believe came from southern China or perhaps Vietnam, showed up around 2000 B.C. In the fifteenth century, the formerly Buddhist Malays converted to Islam. Now, Malays make up about sixty percent of the population. Chinese add another thirty percent. Indians, brought in by the British from all over the subcontinent to work the colonial sugar fields, constitute about ten percent.

The aborigines, called "Negritos" or little black people by the early Europeans and now called Orang Asli or Original People in Malay, are lost in the shuffle. They were here long before the first Malay. Nobody knows exactly how many there are.

Since at least 1948, when Britain carved out the Federation of Malaya from its colonies and protectorates and the British left the sultans nominally in charge, the Malays have been trying to wrest more control from the Chinese, who held most of the economic might. In 1957, the federation gained independence within the British Commonwealth of Nations. On September 16, 1963, Malaysia became a new, independent country by merging the former federation with the states of Sabah and Sarawak on Borneo and the island of Singapore at the tip of the peninsula. Singapore dropped out two years later.

But independence aggravated racial tension. As long as the British were around, no one race was supreme, except the whites of course. But then the white folks left. Racial tension ebbed and flowed until 1969, when murderous riots between Chinese and indians on one side and Malays on the other ripped cities apart. Blood replaced tension. Hundreds died.

Halim was a student then. Some groups wanted him to join. The government was brainwashing him for some unexplained reason. He was being pressured to become a youth leader of gangs attacking Chinese. Finally, he ran away into the jungle. There were secret files about his case in a government office.

"Now," he said conspiratorially into my ear as if a gibbon could be a spy, "nobody knows who I really am."

Actually, that was not completely true. One woman did know who Halim was. She was a Russian. She had come to Taman Negara and Halim had guided her on a walk. They talked.

"She knew many important people," Halim said. "She had contacts in the government and knew about my case."

The woman had left Halim with a copy of *Newsweek*, which he had virtually memorized, and a promise to clear his name. Halim had not heard from the woman for over a year.

"She was working with the KGB, I think," he said. "If anyone could help me, it is her."

Nobody in Malaysia has forgotten the riots, so it is up to the ruling party to keep things together. It starts by trying to control information. In this schizophrenic country, rock bands are free to perform in concert as long as they look like Pat Boone and sing like ABBA. Indeed, one band, a cleaner cut version of Menudo, was banned from television until they cut their hair and wore clothes without rips. The band held a televised hair-cutting ceremony. Malaysia has satellite dishes, but they are outlawed. The minister of information claimed they corrupt the people. He also informed newspapers that it was up to them to uphold government policy.

Officially, Malaysia is a monarchy with the head of state being one of the thirteen sultans who take office in rotation between rounds of golf and marrying wives. In reality, however, Malaysia is run by a political party called UMNO. UMNO is run by a man named Dr. Mahatir bin Mohamad, the nation's prime minister. UMNO stands for United Malay National Organization. A few Malaysians told me it really means "U Must Not Oppose" or "Under Mahatir, No Opposition." It was UMNO's job to keep the country together by walking a tightrope between races, religions, and even sects of religions, specifically Islamic fundamentalists and moderates. UMNO also struggled to keep the sultans in line. Sometimes that meant buying them off with land grants or looking the other way when they misbehaved, like that nasty business when the sultan of Johor was rumored to have murdered his caddy by clubbing him to death with a putter after the caddy chuckled at a missed gimmee.

Mahatir used a nationalist vision to keep the country from flying apart. Mahatir's vision was a kind of Oral-Roberts-and-a-ninety-foot-Jesus-Christ vision. Just as Jesus told Roberts to build a new hospital, despite the glut of beds in Tulsa, Oklahoma, Mahatir's vision told him to increase his country's population and industrialize as fast as possible. He called the program Vision 2020. By the year 2020, he said, Malaysia would be an industrial power. Its population would grow from seventeen million to seventy million. Most of the new people, of course, would be Muslim and racially Malay. The Chinese and indian populations of Malaysia, who were Buddhists, Sikhs, Hindus, Catholics, and a few Baha'is, knew exactly what that meant. Some were checking out real estate in Vancouver.

Vision 2020 became a little like Mao's *Red Book*, a creed Malaysians tried to live by. UMNO was, after all, the government, and the government controlled information within the country. Most Malaysians agreed with Mahatir's goals. They wanted a piece of the First World pie. If trees stood in the way, well, too bad. Trees were one of Malaysia's largest cash generators, cash that could be used to finance the push for industrialization. No matter what the truth about his past, Halim had become an expert, perhaps the only lay expert, on Taman Negara, the Orang Asli, and the forces swirling around the rain forest. Although he had garbled some of the information he had crammed into his head, he was far better read than any other person in the region, and he listened intently to the foreigners he had met.

Like many other rain-forest environments, Taman Negara is deceptive. It is lush and green and even dense at times, but made up of very poor, thin soil. The dirt had been laid down in a thin strip over limestone, so the trees are forced into supporting themselves with massive buttresses sometimes over six feet high. Teak, mahogany, and tualang trees grow to enormous heights. Thick lianas wrap themselves around and between trees. Epiphytes give up on the soil and instead gather nutrients and water from the air and root themselves in host trees. Orchids ranging in size from tiny to gigantic sprout in unexpected places.

But despite the relative infertility of its soil, Taman Negara is a giant storage locker of plant and animal life. There are upward of two hundred tree species in the park, most of them dipterocarp hardwoods especially coveted by lumbermen. Animals ranging from the malaria-carrying anopheles mosquito to Asian elephants could also be found in Taman Negara. But finding a rhino, even with Halim's help, would be difficult.

"I have seen two," Halim reported tantalizingly.

"When was your first one?" I asked.

"About six years ago."

"And your second?"

"About five years ago."

"None since?"

"No. They are very shy and I am not even sure if there are any left in the forest at all. I never see tracks. The people hunt them. The men think the horns are good for female relations."

In fact, actually seeing any large mammals was rare. Tapir, mousedeer (the world's smallest hoofed animal), and civet cats are often spotted, but on our hikes Halim and I saw only the dung of elephants and some old tiger tracks as tantalizing proof that these animals existed in the forest at all. Halim was not disappointed at the scarcity of elephants.

"The elephants are very big, but you sometimes cannot see them. They get frightened if they are surprised and charge. I have been charged many times."

But other animals were scattered all over Taman Negara. Gibbons, macaques, and dozens of bird species kept the forest noisy all day, especially just before dawn and just after sunset. Ringtailed monkeys flitted from tree to tree. The large hornbills, avian rhinos, were everywhere. Eagles swept out of the trees overhanging jungle streams and grabbed small fish from the water.

Halim completely dismissed the idea that snakes could be dangerous. I had run over half a dozen cobras while driving in Malaysia, but Halim insisted he almost never saw one in the jungle.

"Almost?" I asked.

"Well, I have seen some. But they never attack. Just stay away from them and they will not harm you."

That advice seemed sound.

Giant monitor lizards sat by the streams sunning themselves like alligators. As soon as they heard Halim and me walking toward them, they scampered into the water and slithered away.

Nobody knows exactly how many species of insect inhabit the forest, but there may be over one thousand. We watched three-foot-long centipedes roam the forest floor looking for smaller prey. The most famous butterfly in Asia, the Rajah Brooke's birdwing, a giant black-and-green beauty as big as a man's hand, fluttered head high, in an apparition. But all the insects were wary of the fearsome army ants whose movement through the undergrowth sounded like thousands of tiny clicks everywhere we walked.

These ants, moving in streams of millions, are organized like Patton's march through Europe. Columns of workers are guarded by larger sargeants who keep the line moving, discipline strays, and attack intruders. They are capable of stripping meat off a bone in minutes and can theoretically kill a man with bites that leave the ants' heads embedded in the skin if the man sits still for it.

A man does not have to sit still for the leeches. Halim and I walked toward a river backwater that had formed into a large pool in the forest. The land all around the pool was filled with leeches. In fact, it was virtually impossible to walk anywhere in Taman Negara without finding a tiny pink Slinky inching its way up a sock, hunting for warm blood. There were only two courses of action, to keep a constant lookout and never see anything else in the forest, or let them eat. Halim opted to let them eat. I, on the other hand, did not consider myself an Asian Jesus, so it took me a few days to stop looking for the little vampires every few feet.

At least they made unobtrusive guests. They injected a tiny painkiller into the wound they made and added a blood thinner so it could be very difficult to know if a leech was attached. When we found one, we pulled it off, releasing a tiny drop of blood that trickled down our legs.

Taman Negara's limestone base was ripe for cave formations. There were several in the park. Late one afternoon Halim led me to Gua Telinga, Little Ear, a cave and a rock outcropping down a heavily forested slope. Gua Telinga was home to hundreds of bats, the cave racer snake that fed on the bats, and the huge cave frog that fed on the insects that fed on bat droppings.

Halim and I sat outside the cave for a few minutes. We could hear the bats inside, but it was too early for their nightly departure. Halim asked if I wanted to climb in.

"Is there room?" I wanted to know before committing.

"Oh yes, there is lots of room," he said perpetrating a lie unbecoming a jungle philosopher.

Halim led the way in. Within two meters of the cave entrance we had to fall flat on our bellies to squeeze through the narrow space between two rock ledges. We were immediately covered in bat guano. It was several inches thick over parts of the cave floor. I kept reminding myself that bats have really, really, good radar. They hardly ever run into anything. And insects eat bat shit. It was natural. It was life.

None of this rationalization worked. Crawling through Gua Telinga on my stomach and my back was gooey, and there was no romanticizing it. Still, when we reached a small cavern with about three feet of clearance, we could crouch and watch the bats, hundreds of them clinging to the cave walls and ceiling, some in small groups, some beating their wings and flying to other spots on the rock. They brushed by our heads, and a few touched our bodies, sending a spine rattle up the back of my neck. And yet, after a few minutes, I began to trust their radar, trust they would not send their little black bodies hurtling into my skull like a hot-rodding teenager after a six-pack.

The tourists who came to Taman Negara skipped the Gua Telinga bat-shit ride. They preferred the jungle rivers, like the Tahan, that run down from the cloud forests and into the lowlands. These jungle streams flow under green arches made by the branches of trees on either bank that intertwine to create a kind of leafy lace.

The Europeans liked a rocky rapids called Latah Berkoh. There, they walked out on the rocks, stripped off their clothes, and lay in the middle of the river as the water flowed over their bodies, washing away the First World. I asked the boatmen why they thought this happened. They were not sure why the German women always took their clothes off and sat in the river, but they did not much care, either. The sight sure beat the Mercury outboard calendar. I watched the young Muslim boys sit in their T-shirts and whisper among themselves and smile goofy grins. I liked the irony of the naked Europeans trying to touch a piece of the primitive jungle while the locals fantasized about touching a piece of the Europeans.

After a week of walking and hiking around Taman Negara, I was beginning to despair of any rain-forest revelation. There would be no rhino sighting. And if the people I had met had their way, they would be living in condos.

The Orang Asli did not seem too far behind, though they were just catching on. For a few, the world was still in the Stone Age. They collected poisoned sap from the *ara bertih* tree, treated their darts with it, and hunted gibbon, macaque, and wild hogs with blowguns. They lived in thatched lean-tos, moving from place to place in small family groups. They left everybody else alone and preferred to avoid visitors. But some groups had decided to live semipermanently on the forest's fringes. It would not be long before they were joined by their brothers in the interior. The Orang Asli way of life was dying.

The government, the government told me in a prepared statement, was providing for the Orang Asli. It was taking them from the forests, from the places where they had roamed nomadically and hunted and collected fruits for millenia, and was placing them in new "villages." The villages were made of concrete block.

Sometimes the aborigines protested being moved, saying thank you for trying to provide for us, but we prefer the forest to the concrete blocks. But even this was not completely a pure emotion. Westerners had come, especially to Borneo, and had made the tribes face what they stood to lose. A few tribes had P.R. agents. The government picked up on the western activist presence and used the whites as bogeymen, blaming unrest among the natives on "radical environmentalists. . . . The Malaysian government makes no apology for helping seminomadic and nomadic groups living in the fringe and within the jungles to lead settled lives. . . . " All for their own good, naturally.

The government wanted the Orang Asli out of the forest in part for reasons of religion and progress. The Orang Asli are not Muslim. They are roughly equivalent to animists. They are also something of an embarrassment. Since most are illiterate and live such crude lives, they stand as a reminder of Malaysia's past when the country was backward. It was tough to square skyscrapers in Kuala Lumpur with grub-eating, thatched-roof-living black natives. So, the government was sending the Orang Asli to its concrete Potemkin Villages, where they could farm one plot of land. This despite the Orang Asli's millennia of wandering as nomads in the forest, hunting and gathering.

Of course, the government also had another purpose. The Orang Asli lived in forests, and the forests were being logged about as fast as Malaysia could log them. In Sarawak, on Borneo, the Penan tribe blocked logging roads and engaged in civil disobedience. But that was on Borneo.

The "original people" of Taman Negara thought they had found easy street.

The *tok batin* of the tiny village hidden away on the bank of the Tembeling south of Kuala Tahan wasn't aware of politics. He also wasn't aware of his name and was a little fuzzy on his age. When I asked his name through Halim, he looked puzzled for a second because he was, simply, the *tok batin*, or headman. Then it dawned on him what I was looking for. He smiled, happy to be able to satisfy my request, and dashed into a hut. He returned with a small weathered identity card issued by the government, referred to it studiously, and announced that his name was Keladong bin Bulat. It was clearly a name he wasn't used to. It had been given to him in adulthood by the government. As for his age, the card suggested he should be sixty-seven. That looked close enough.

According to Halim, Keladong and his group of about fifty people walked out of the forest one day to settle semipermanently by the river. They learned to speak Malay. They welcomed tourists, few of whom actually came to the village. They called the tourists "friends." They also welcomed the government agent who brought them meals in styrofoam trays.

I asked the *tok batin* how the people liked living here. Didn't they miss the old life? Didn't they find "friends" intrusive and annoying or the government agent with his meals too aggressive? I believe the *tok batin* had to restrain himself from laughing. He very patiently explained the facts of life. "I am so happy people come to visit us. We can meet new friends, new people. This is a good thing." He popped a piece of candy Halim had brought into his mouth and smiled a toothless smile.

"Making friends is the most important thing. We like to give them gifts. Sometimes friends give gifts or food to us. We like the food they bring."

Essentially, Keladong was saying to this very dense friend, "What? You think it's fun trudging through the forest hunting monkeys and digging up roots? I don't see you tracking an ape for three hours. The government shows up with food, ready to eat. There's a problem here?"

As he talked, he pointed to a black plastic watch on his wrist. Its liquid-crystal face was obscured with dirt. The watch did not work and had not worked in a long time. It may never have worked. (According to Halim, the Orang Asli liked cassette tape players but did not think they were built very well. They did not last long. The concept of changing batteries had not quite caught on.)

"We are more settled, yes," he continued. "This is better." He described how they still gathered tapioca and bananas and sold some of these to the makeshift floating stores that lined the river's edge near Malay villages.

The tiny community was littered with the fruits of their labor. Plastic jugs, empty soda bottles, cellophane candy wrappers, and cigarette packages were scattered everywhere. The Orang Asli almost always spent their money at the store to which they sold the fruits. They bought candy and snack foods. Their only square meals came from the government. Just before we had arrived, the government agent had delivered a meal in trays like those used for Italian take-out. The Orang Asli, of course, had nowhere to put the trays when they were finished. The river was a sea of styrofoam.

Their diet had changed so much and they had such a taste for junk food and candy, Halim said, that even young men were often unable to make the trek to the 7,100 foot peak of Gunung Tahan, a mountain that was the highest point in peninsular Malaysia. In the past, they had made that hike regularly.

While capitalism had been born, private property was still a wild idea. The village was communal. While each family had a lean-to or an elevated thatched hut, children ran in and out of huts and adults wandered inside dwellings not their own to look for a plastic jug or a knife or a stick. Most of the men gathered in a communal smoking place to talk and chew betel that turned their lips and teeth a brilliant red. The Orang Asli wore clothes, sort of, but they were not sticklers about it. They were also not sticklers about government. To them, the government was the guy who brought the food. The government also appointed a young man, Dayak, as the official *tok batin*. Dayak got a shirt and a badge with his name on it. He was very proud of his shirt and his badge. He had no authority. Keladong went right on being *tok batin*. Dayak did not seem to mind. He had his shirt.

While the Orang Asli were not sticklers for much of anything, the local Muslims were. Kelantan, in the northeastern corner of the country, enacted fundamentalist laws and established Islamic courts. Theoretically the laws are applicable only to Muslims within the state, but groups of Muslims throughout the north and central parts of the peninsula make no secret of their desire to emulate Kelantan and turn Malaysia into a nation governed by *shariah* law like that enforced in Iran.

Most Malays doubt such a thing could ever happen. Malaysia has certainly given a strong nod to Islam, and some of its laws are based on the religion. But Malays are Asian with a strong tradition of friendliness, openess, and casual living. In mosques throughout most of Malaysia, Malay women dress in colorful sarongs, often without their heads covered. Alcohol is served throughout the country, although Muslims are not supposed to drink it. Malaysia practices Islam with a smile.

But the push for Islamic law was on and it had come to Taman Negara. Local Muslim leaders were convinced that the Orang Asli must become Muslim.

During a hike searching for the rhino, Halim seemed agitated. I asked what was wrong.

"I have to go to an important meeting with the imams," he said with a look that said Halim had no taste for meetings, nor for imams.

"What about?"

"They say the Orang Asli are not leading Muslim lives. They want them to go to Muslim schools, leave the forest."

A few hours later, as we trudged through the forest back toward the Tembeling, we came across half a dozen lean-tos.

"Orang Asli," Halim said.

The dwellings had been abandoned for a month or so. They had been built by a small family group, possibly hunters going after monkeys. Most likely, the lean-tos had been a base for the hunters, who had since returned to their more permanent homes deeper in the jungle. Halim sighed. Soon you would not be able to find the impromptu homes any more. He knew that the days of Orang Asli in Taman Negara were numbered. During his sojourns in the jungle, Halim had relied on Orang friends to show him how to survive, and they did. He had become close to even remote family groups that had little contact with the outside world. He did not want to see them tamed.

At the meeting between the Orang Asli government agent, regional Muslim officials, and Halim, the Muslims asked Halim how long it would take to convert the Orang Asli. Halim laughed, a reaction the Muslims did not find amusing. Halim tried to explain that culturally, the Orang Asli are as far removed from the philosophy of Islam as it is possible to get. There is no religious hierarchy, no church, no God as Muslims (or Christians or Jews for that matter) conceive of God. For the Orang Asli, the forest is alive, the trees and rivers sentient. You did not need a god when you could talk to the plants.

The government agent piped up that the Orang Asli could begin to be assimilated in school, which they would, of course, have to attend sometime soon. Halim laughed again. The Orang Asli, he said, had no conception of time divided in increments smaller than morning, evening, night, and the next day. Keeping an appointment with an Orang Asli amounted to saying you would meet in the morning. The idea of convincing groups of Orang Asli to appear at a school building at 8:00 every morning was out of the question as far as Halim was concerned. "It could never be done," he insisted.

Halim knew very little about the history of the American indian.

The next morning Halim and I sat at a table at the park's lodge and ate some curry. The lodge manager, who knew Halim well, sat down with us. We talked about the meeting the night before. Halim was still disturbed.

"But those people are ignorant," the manager said. "They do not know anything. They are always hanging around here looking for handouts. They ought to be educated."

The manager was a porcine young man who was raised in Kuala Lumpur and could not wait until the company that owned the lodge transferred him back out of the jungle and into a nice businessman's hotel in the city. He toed the UMNO party line. Progress was necessary. There was the park. The rain forest would be saved. The rest of the jungles could go as far as he was concerned. Malaysia could not be kept down by westerners.

"I suppose you do not think we should cut any trees," he said, challenging me.

But I had already learned my lesson about discussing timber with Malaysians. I had followed caravans of lumber trucks on narrow, winding roads as they left clear-cut hillsides so overloaded with huge logs that the drivers had actually gone on strike to protest unsafe conditions. Saying anything negative about this, though, was an invitation to a lecture on how the CIA had been stirring up trouble among the Orang Asli and Borneo tribes like the Penan and how environmentalism was a front to keep Malaysia down.

Malaysians were so sensitive to the issue because the country was often beat up in the international press. So, to counter the pounding Malaysia was getting in the West, the government handed out literature to visiting journalists showing that seventy percent of the country was covered by trees. That was true. On the other hand, most of the peninsula had been logged and natural forest replaced by palm oil and rubber plantations. The government counted that as tree cover. And in the Borneo states of Sarawak and Sabah, vast tracts had been denuded by logging. In fact, the government did not want journalists going to Sarawak, which required an internal visa. To get there, a reporter had to lie and risk arrest.

Still, the pressure had forced the government to moderate its policy a little. For example, it allowed more international research in the jungles and set aside some significant acreage on Borneo for preservation. In 1991, tree-girth restrictions were imposed to limit logging to more mature trees while leaving younger trees standing.

None of that, of course, meant that the Orang Asli would stay in the jungle.

So I deflected the conversation to the anniversary then being celebrated, the Prophet's birthday, a national holiday. I had been invited to attend a special service at the mosque in Kuala Tahan. A talk would by given by a very holy imam. The manager and Halim and I made plans to attend together.

As night began to fall, the bell on the tiny timber mosque rang, and villagers carrying flashlights to illuminate the dirt path walked toward the frame house of worship.

"I will be interested to see what you think of this group," Halim told me. "They are being hunted by the government."

Well, not exactly, as it turned out. Officially banned and discouraged was more like it, but they still traveled to rural mosques like this one and preached their message, the message of the House of Al-Arqam.

Small children dressed in colorful pants and tunics and mini-fezes scrambled over the porch that encircled the mosque. Inside, their fathers prayed and then sat with crossed legs to listen to the preacher. Their mothers sat on the floor behind white screens at the rear of the congregation. Three women were dressed in full black chadors in defiance of the warm night. The rest of the women wore white or bright floral patterns, with scarves on their heads. Although a few women listened carefully, most talked and gossiped.

Meanwhile Halim paced nervously outside. Although a Muslim, he was not dressed in the typical loose-fitting trousers and long tunic. He wore his daily uniform of sweatpants and T-shirt. He did not join the others inside the mosque. I felt sorry for him. Somehow, I thought, the crossroads running through Taman Negara were running through Halim's head, too, and now there was no place for him—not with the Muslims, or the Orang Asli, or even the Malays. He was as isloated as the park surrounded by clear-cuts.

A cherubic man, the self-appointed music director for the children, sat down next to me on the porch. Children, distracted from what was a loose service anyway, spotted me, too. Like most other Malaysians who did not speak English, they knew the same few words. "Hey, Joe," they said. "Where you from?"

The choir director explained that the visiting holy men were very strict Muslims. The preacher was telling his audience to be friends with unbelievers and that Islamic people fighting each other, as in the Middle East, was a terrible thing.

"Even infidels can be our friends!" the choir director exclaimed joyfully. Then he bowed his head seriously. His Malaysian culture had run smack into his Islamic fervor. "I am very sorry," he said. "I did not mean to insult you by calling you an infidel."

"I'm not insulted," I assured him.

He smiled sweetly, happy I was not offended.

"Well," he continued with renewed excitement, "The imam is telling us that big shots and kings can be told they are not right and that the government should not interfere."

"In what?" I asked.

"In our lives. Our laws and rules should be based on Islam, not government."

After the service was over, the congregation gathered on the porch for a meal. Young boys and teenagers rolled out long green mats and placed cups and silver water pitchers shaped like tea kettles in circles arranged about six feet apart. The young imam who had been preaching approached me. Halim was by his side, as were the manager of the lodge and the superintendent of Taman Negara. Two of the imam's aides were with him. The women were gathered on the other side of the mosque.

The imam was dressed in a long green gown. A turban topped his head. He wore the beginnings of a beard. His aides dressed identically. No other people that night wore turbans or beards. I learned later that wearing green and wearing a beard were considered holy acts by the leader of Al-Arqam, Ustaz Asha'ari Muhammad. At first I thought the teacher was over thirty, but as we talked, I realized he could not have been more than twenty-three or twenty-four. Yet he struggled to carry himself with great severity. His name was Edris and he was from Jerantut, a town near Kuala Tembeling where I had boarded the boat for Taman Negara. A boy held the silver water container above a silver bowl, and following the lead of the others, I washed my right hand as he poured the water over it. A big pot of rice was placed in the middle of our group, and smaller bowls of chicken, beef, and vegetables were placed before us. We scooped the rice followed by the other selections, onto plates. The left hand being unholy, we ate with our right.

Between bites and much finger licking, Edris spoke with all the assurance of a man who was convinced he had the answers. Inside all of us, he said, there was a Muslim wanting out. The way to get the Muslim out of each of us was to follow the word of Mohammad and the teachings of Ustaz Asha'ari.

"There is only salvation in Islam," he explained. "You in the West are infidels and cannot be saved because you do not follow Mohammad." But even Edris had to fight his upbringing. "I am sorry, please do not take offense when I call you an infidel."

"I'm not offended," I said. "I'm about as infidel as you can get. What you are saying sounds very familiar to me."

"You see, we believe that the only way to achieve salvation is to accept Allah as your God and to follow His laws. That is why I dress this way. It is a higher form of dress than that of the others," he said indicating my fellow diners. "We must return to the old values. There are too many influences from outside, and these are corrupting our people."

"Like allowing Muslim men to have four wives?" I asked.

"Yes. We must teach the women about this. Then they will get used to it."

I explained that his words sounded a lot like a group of people we have in the United States. "We call these people fundamentalist Christians," I said. "They believe you are an infidel and that you cannot have salvation unless you become Christian. Who do you think is right?"

"We are right. There is only Allah."

Later, Edris gave me a book called *This Is Our Way*, written by Ustaz Asha'ari. It was a declaration of the group's tenets and its antipathy for the government which had decided that Vision 2020 and old-time religion did not mix. The book also declared that the most dangerous enemies of Islam after Satan and a Muslim's baser self were Communists, Jews, Zoroastrians, and Christians. He described the twelve obstacles to a true Islamic world. They included political parties, other ideologies, free thinking, and "yellow culture"—in other words, Western and Japanese influences that "are proud of free mixing among the sexes," which was a "weird lifestyle."

The other men in the group listened deferentially. But it seemed they decided that while Edris may be holier, he was not much fun. After the meal, the lodge manager and the superintendent and I walked down to the river bank in the dark, talking about the imam and the service. The manager poked me in the ribs.

"Now remember, Brian. When you see a girl, no matter how beautiful, don't ever think about kissing her." He belly-laughed all the way to the dock.

When we arrived at the other side of the river, the manager invited me to his cabin to share some durian with the superintendent and the imam and his entourage. I knew that this moment, a quintessentially tropical Asian experience, would come eventually. I gulped hard and accepted gratefully.

Durian, a fruit that grows wild throughout tropical Asia, is a delicacy, expensive by Malaysian standards. When someone offers to crack open a durian, he is honoring his guest with the best he has. This was the manager's tribute to the imam. But durian is unlike any other fruit. Signs in finer hotels in Malaysia say this: "No dead fish or durian allowed in the rooms." Durian's aroma had hints of unwashed jockstrap and animal dung.

"Eating durian is like finding heaven in a sewer," the manager said.

The fruit is about the size of a small pineapple. It is spiked on the outside. When it is split open, the two halves reveal compartments in which seeds the size of a baby's fist are nestled. One eats durian by picking up these seeds, holding one between the thumb and fingers, and sucking the soft, creamy meat off it.

As we all sat around a table filled with small cakes, mineral water, and cans of Coke, the manager cracked open the durian for his guests. I was assaulted by the smell. But despite being repelled, there was no way I was going to back down from durian. It was thought to have evolved in the rain forests of Malaysia, where it was called King of Fruits, so I was eating from the source. And besides, I was sitting in front of a man who had just called me an infidel.

I grabbed a seed, looked at the eyes in the room, and bit off as much meat as I could manage. The imam smiled. His aides saw the imam smile, and they smiled. Everybody else smiled. So I smiled, trying to hide the fact I was about to retch. With smell and taste so intimately connected, I was unable to separate the two. Durian, with its onionlike flavor and athletic-supporter aroma, would be an acquired taste.

When it came the imam's turn, he poured a glass of Coke. It was rumored that Coke drunk after eating durian produces a slight narcotic affect. I wondered if the imam was trying to get around the Islamic rules. If so, it seemed to me, a good Scotch would have been much better.

We sat and talked between bites of durian and sips of Coke. The three women, one of whom turned out to be Edris' sister, sat in their black chadors at another table talking quietly. They were not permitted to sit with the men. We discussed the forest and the Orang Asli, who, Edris said, should be taught Muslim ways. The superintendent was very quiet. He knew Taman Negara as well as Halim, and he loved it. But he also knew that there was a good chance that people like Edris would some day became more powerful. If that day came, the forest would take a back seat to fervor. He could not decide whether to laugh at Edris' pomposity or fear the possibility that young men like Edris would become a real force in the country. He sat staring at Edris and silently asking himself about the deliberate reversal of time.

The following day, my last morning in Taman Negara, I woke early with the taste of durian still on my tongue and hiked into the forest. The gibbons were just waking up. Mousedeer scrambled on the trail ahead of me. Pheasant rummaged in the underbrush.

Wild pigs snorted as they searched for roots. And at my feet, the army ants marched and marched, clicking their mandibles.

The sun rose after an hour or so, and I started back to the lodge. A few yards out of the forest, I ran into Edris and his entourage. They were going hiking. He was dressed in his long gown and turban. His aides were dressed in their long gowns and turbans. The women were dressed in their black chadors. Only their eyes showed. It was 7:30 A.M. It was ninety degrees.

I returned to my cabin and packed up my gear, preparing to meet the boat that would take me back down the river. It took me about twenty minutes. I came out of my room with my bag and ran into Edris and company. He had unbuttoned the top of his gown. The women pulled their chadors in and out, trying to generate a little breeze. They were all sweating. The hike was over. The forest had won. Today.

I walked to the stairs that led down to the dock. A few feet from the stairs a young Orang Asli man sat under some trees wearing only dirty shorts and a smile.

GONNA RAIN LIKE HELL
(ALASKA)

"Gonna rain like hell," Joe Willy said for the umpteenth time. This time, though, I believed him. I could see the black sky over the hanging glaciers near the confluence of the Tatshenshini and the Alsek rivers and could smell the change in the weather roiling up the valley. The river valley formed a natural wind tunnel from the Pacific coast of Alaska into the St. Elias Mountains to British Columbia, where we happened to be at the moment, and it was sending the weather right at us.

Joe Willy, a tall, bearded Georgian and his lover, Kelly, a tiny blonde woman who was strong as an ox, had been promising rain from the morning we put the rafts into the Tatshenshini in the Yukon Territory. I didn't believe them. The sky was blue and the air was warm. The next morning, as I ran out of the woods with my pants around my ankles to escape a moose that had intruded on my morning routine, they said it again. Again it did not rain. But as the river flowed out of high tundra and aspen forests and down toward the coastal mountains, I began to think they were right.

And they were.

The most miserable weather in the world may exist in southeast Alaska and the Haines Triangle region of British Columbia, the section of the province that hangs down like a tooth into U.S. territory and contains the two wild rivers. The "Tat" and the Alsek, fed by melting glaciers, ran just above freezing. The wind swirling up the valley lashed at skin, turned the constant damp into bone-chilling air, and transformed camp meals into gritty stews. That was on good days. But the region also contained some of the most rugged, primeval, spectacular scenery on the planet. The river valley included the most heavily glaciated mountains outside the polar regions. Grizzly bear rumbled through the misty woods. The black bear and its blue brother the glacier bear swam in the river, walked over the glaciers, and foraged for berries. Dall sheep, mountain goats, wolves, bald eagle, mink, marmots, ducks, and salmon lived in and around the rivers and the forests. And, as I had discovered, there were moose, too.

"There is such an incessant display of scenic wild granduer," wrote explorer Edward Glave in 1890, "that it became tiresome. We can no longer appreciate it; its awe-inspiring influence no longer appeals to our hardened senses." Albert Bierstadt could never have imagined the Tatshenshini, one of the last utterly wild places of North America, a place one hundred miles from the nearest road.

The fact that somebody wanted to build a road was, indirectly, what brought me here. A mining company planned to create one of the largest copper mines in the world in the heart of the wilderness near the confluence of the Alsek and Tatshenshini. The firm would put in the road, it said, and eventually place two hundred million tons of waste rock behind a huge earthern dam that the company hoped would contain the leeching acids from the tailings. Rock that did not go in the dam would be dumped on a glacier. Some of the Canadian First Nations, like the Champagne-Aishihik band, were in favor of the mine. They had invested in heavy equipment just in time to experience a Yukon depression. The machinery sat rusting on tribal lands. The mine would mean money and jobs and pride.

Environmentalists on both sides of the U.S.-Canada border were opposed to the mine. If the acid leaked, they said, the rivers would die. Alaska's Glacier Bay National Park would be forever damaged. The fisheries would be destroyed. And the wilderness would be ruined forever. Why not declare the region protected, link it with Kluane National Park in the Yukon, Wrangell-St. Elias National Park to the north in Alaska, and Glacier Bay? The combined parks would create the largest protected area on the face of the earth.

Suddenly a remote place everyone had ignored for a very long time became an eco epicenter. The U.S. Congress passed resolutions, songs were sung, pictures were painted, and very annoying environmentalists shrilled slogans.

Amy was one of these. She and her boyfriend were young activists for the Tat, the kind of conservationists reminiscent of weeping religious seers. She and Tom treated me to several sermons not only on the Tatshenshini controversy but also on Clayoquot, the temperate rain forest near Vancouver that the British Columbia government was about to open for logging. Amy could not talk about such things without tearing up. She teared up a lot.

The first time I met Amy, she objected to the presence of a rifle in the raft.

"Why are we bringing that?" she challenged Joe Willy.

"Bears," he said in about as concise an answer as anyone needed in this region of bears.

"You will not shoot a bear with that," she said not really phrasing it as a question.

"If I have to," Joe Willy replied.

"I can't believe you would actually shoot an animal."

"Well how about I let any bears chewing on you go right ahead and only shoot if one is chewing on somebody else. Okay?"

Relations disintegrated from there.

One night Amy led a long campfire discussion on why we should not be burying our shit and burning our toilet paper, but rather packing it out with our other trash. The presence of human feces, she said, would disrupt the balance of nature, introduce human germs, and turn the pristine river valley and the mountains into a sewer. She painted a picture worse than the slums of Calcutta. A giant pile of bear scat sat three feet away, deposited there by some wandering grizzly a few days before.

"How many bears do you think live around here?" I asked. "And how often do you think they shit in the woods?"

This only made her angry. We clearly did not deserve to be in this place, she said. We did not appreciate nature. We were defilers, despoilers, desecraters. And when Joe Willy tossed some lettuce leaves into the river, well, she knew for sure she was rafting with barbarians. All the pointing at the giant trees that had fallen off the banks into the river, dropping their dead leaves into the water, could not mollify her. She ranted and pouted and cried, even, at how we were whipping the great mother of us all. Tom put his arms around her, comforted her, and said he understood. It was painful to see such behavior, Tom said. They stomped off in their Birkenstocks to their tent and never spoke to us again. Which was not such a bad thing.

We reached a small island in the confluence where the Tat flowed into the Alsek and the ecosystem began to look more and more like temperate coastal rain forest. The weather began to disintegrate. Hard little drops poured out of the sky. I asked Joe Willy if it was, in fact, raining like hell.

"Not yet," he shouted back from his oars. "Not enough angle."

A few minutes later, though, the angle had improved. Wind was driving the rain into us at sixty degrees. The drops actually hurt. The conditions made setting up tents virtually impossible.

That amused Ron Chambers. He stood on the small island where we had beached, petted his husky, sipped his coffee, and laughed. He was here, he said, with an archaeologist hired by the indians to examine some glyphs that had been carved in rocks on the island. If the glyphs could be identified as coming from the Tutchone people, the precursors to the band, the Champagne-Aishihik might be able to claim the land under a provision of the Canadian constitution.

Ron, an indian himself and a ranger at Kluane, said the band didn't quite understand the conservationist view. Some members did not necessarily want the mine, he said, but they did not agree with the upper-middle-class white people who came up from cities like Vancouver and New York and Los Angeles and stood in romantic awe of the place. Came just to see it. indians were more practical.

"They have a hard time with people just going into the wilderness without a purpose," he said. "They see land as different from that. They don't think it should be just set aside."

Over the final three days of the expedition I thought about Ron and the indian view. When I woke in the mornings and climbed out of my tent and into the cold air, I looked at the mists in the trees. I watched the brief glimpse of the sun beam off the blue ice of a glacier that tumbled in giant frozen falls out of the mountains. I watched the bear walk across the glacier, using it as a highway instead of fighting the thick brush by the river. Another bear fought to cross the rushing waters of the Alsek three times before giving up and realizing that life on his own side of the river might not be so bad. We hiked onto the glacier and listened to the moulins, the icy sapphire holes with minitaure rivers corkscrewing through them, creating a network of tunnels. We hiked up a snow-covered hill called The Nose once we passed out of Canada and into Glacier Bay National Park. At the top, wildflowers, whose life expectancy was a week or so before it came time to hibernate again, had bloomed and dotted the hillside. Finally, tired, wet, cold, and having long since given up all pretense of personal hygiene, we floated into Alsek Lake, a wide spot in the river maybe a mile across. Through the mist we could see a huge glacier pouring down off Mt. Root, a 12,860-foot peak. The glacier had split in two around a much smaller mountain and formed separate frozen rivers that calved off the icebergs floating lazily in the water. We paddled to a spot in the Tongass National Forest on the north side of the lake and set up our tents for the last time.

The mist began to lift, and the clouds rose higher in the sky. A few escaped rays of the sun bounced off our tents, and we paid attention. We all stood like schoolchildren waiting for Fireman Rick to show off his truck. As the late-afternoon sun dipped below the clouds, it bounced off the glaciers on the other side of the lake, turning them brilliant hues of blue and white. The clouds lifted higher and higher, and we could just see the lower half of Mt. Fairweather's snow-covered peak to the south.

Joe Willy and Kelly had rafted everywhere. They annually packed up their truck in the Alaskan autumn and drove it to Costa Rica where they rafted rain forest rivers during the winter. They had rafted Africa's Zambezi, Chile's Bio Bio, Idaho's Middle Fork of the Salmon—all the majestic rivers of the world. They had rafted the Tat and the Alsek a dozen times.

Joe Willy and Kelly stood and stared, and none of us said a word for a long time.

The clouds lifted completely. We could see all 15,300 feet of Mt. Fairweather. We could see the forest, the glaciers, the lake. And that night, unable to sleep and not really wanting to, I could poke my head out of my tent and see stars and the Northern Lights and the glow of the glaciers, and I could hear the roar of new icebergs being born and baptized in the cold water.

I have never seen the Taj Mahal. I have never seen the Pyramids or Picasso's *Guernica* or the cave paintings at Lascaux. I might never see them. But I knew they are there, serving no practical purpose.

YES, WE HAVE NO DENGUE TODAY
(GUATEMALA)

We had been in Guatemala's Petén rain forest only a few minutes when Don Lanzas held his machete against a tree, snapped off a little bark, and smiled a wide, nearly toothless grin that crinkled his face into deep canyons of lines. Then he laughed and looked at me, sizing me up.

"This," he said with a sly look in his eyes that told me he was about to mention women or sex or both, "will turn you into a machine."

I tried some. Just to be polite, of course. Later, I would try some more in a café. I mean, you never knew about these folk medicines. But at the moment I had to wonder what it was about me that seemed to cry out for arboreal potency boosters. I was working up a midsized complex over this when suddenly, out of the tree tops, a troop of spider monkeys began hurling fruit at us with the accuracy of a short relief pitcher. Don Lanzas swore and held his machete up in the air, rattling saber and threatening the monkeys.

Thwap! Don Lanzas was hit in the back. Knowing when he was beaten, he jogged away, farther into the Petén's deep forest, a forest he first entered at the age of twelve, over fifty years before.

Back then, Don Lanzas was a *chiclero*, a collector of chicle, the milky latex sap used as a base for chewing gum. Back then, most of the gum in the world used chicle as a base, and you could make a respectable living as a chicle tapper, carving diagonal grooves in the *zapote* trees, collecting the sap, processing the gum into bricks and shipping it off. So, when Don Lanzas was twelve, his mother took him out of school and sent him into the forest.

The fact that he survived was something of a miracle. The work was brutal. Fer-de-lance and coral snakes, two of the deadliest snakes in the world, hid under tree roots and leaves. And *chicleros* were notorious tough guys. They drank hard; got laid in the crowded, muddy, Calle Rojo in Santa Elena; and drunkenly dueled each other with their machetes. It wasn't unusual, Don Lanzas said, for two men to go into the forest together to work and have only one come back.

"The one that came back would always say the other one got lost or walked away and that was all. Nobody asked any questions."

To this day, he said, some *chicleros* would kill you for a few *quetzales*.

Now Don Lanzas worked for Mayarema. Don Lanzas was being

paid to tell the scientists working for Mayarema what he knew about the plants in the forest. Don Lanzas thought this was a very good thing. It sure beat collecting chicle. There were thirty-two separate organizations in the Petén all trying to help Don Lanzas, most funded by the U.S. Agency for International Development— US AID, the mother acronym. There was CARE, WCI, and ProPetén and CATIE. There was RENARM and ROCAP and CECON. The Peace Corps was here and so was The Nature Conservancy, and the ultimate BMOC of all these acronyms was a man named Alfredo Nakatsuma. Yessir, between the Mayan site looters, smugglers, government soldiers, leftist rebels, archaeologsts, biologists, conservationists, and aid workers—well, brother, the Petén was hopping. Don Lanzas thought this was a very good thing indeed. He stood under a big mahogany safely away from the monkeys and laughed and laughed, his belly popping the buttons on his dirty old shirt.

In Guatemala City, the Petén seems very far away. But then, in the relatively well-to-do Zona 9 section of town, the glue sniffing kids in the *colonias* around the corner can seem far away. For a city so wedged among spectacular volcanic mountains, Guatemala City is a homely place. This is partly because it is home to at least ten percent of the country's booming population. In 1973, the estimated population of the city was about 750,000. Now it is about 1.5 million. The influx has made the city overcrowded, and sometimes violent. And the city was virtually destroyed by earthquakes in the early 1900s and had to be rebuilt, a process that replaced Spanish colonial buildings with cheap versions of modern ones.

But you can get good coffee in Guatemala City, especially in Zona 9. I sat sipping the dark ambrosia in a sidewalk cafe after calling the U.S. Embassy, which, not coincidentally, was also located in Zona 9. When I called, I asked for Alfred Nakatsuma. I had made arrangements to speak with Alfred long before coming to

Guatemala. Alfred was a natural resources expert with US AID. But behind that innocuous title was an important man.

I had first heard of Alfred Nakatsuma when I happened to see an astonishing photograph taken from a NASA satellite. When satellites take pictures that include more than one country, you can never see borders. Borders are black lines drawn on maps. They do not exist in nature. Except for the border between the Petén and Mexico. The border there, shown in the photograph, was as sharply defined as any black line on a map. In the picture, the Mexican side is brown, stark, shaved like a marine's head. The Petén is green, lush, with only a few brown spots showing through. At the time, I wondered if I was looking at a mirror of the future.

So I learned more about el Petén and as I learned, the name Alfred Nakatsuma kept surfacing from under the facts and figures. I had, I thought, a great idea for a story. It would be a story about the place and about Alfred in that place. And in doing the story, I hoped Alfred, who I imagined was a little like me, could apply some Rosetta Stone of understanding to the puzzles that kept me going to jungles.

It was a story that would never happen. Alfred wasn't at the embassy when I called. Someone said to leave my number. He would call back. So I sat in the café and watched the black-leather crowd stroll by and look in shop windows. The jungle seemed very far away. This was Miami.

When I returned to my room, there was a message from the embassy. Alfred was sorry. He had to go into the north, into the Petén, for an important meeting. Maybe we could work something out?

I called back and spoke to a secretary who knew little English and became easily frustrated at my slow Spanish.

"*Alfredo no esta aqui.*"

"*Sí, entiendo. Pero, tengo una cita con Alfredo. Soy una periodista de los Estados Unidos.*"

Having just told the secretary—in a somewhat pleading, whiny voice—that I was a journalist from the United States who had a date with Alfredo, as in movie and dinner and a little wine at my place, it was no wonder she paused a long time.

She tried ignoring the issue and speaking English.

"Yesss," she said slowly. "Alfredo is no here."

"I know he's not there. I have a message that he went to Petén, but we had an appointment. To talk."

"But he will be in el Petén two day."

"I am going to Petén in two days."

"No, he is already in Petén. He left this morning."

"I know, yes, *sí, entiendo*. Alfredo is in Petén. I will be in Petén in two days. *Voy ir a Petén en dos días más, sí?*"

"*Sí.*"

"Can Alfredo wait for me there, in Petén? I want to see him in Petén."

"Alfredo is in Petén."

The secretary and I duked it out for several more rounds like two palookas at a county fair until it became clear that Alfredo could not wait for me in Petén. There were Germans coming to Guatemala City. They were government bureaucrats. Since Germany was a contributor to Alfred's project to save the rain forest, Mayarema, they were coming to see how the German people's money was being spent. Alfredo was needed in the city. I left a message, doubtful it would ever reach Alfredo, that I hoped to see him in Petén. If not, I wanted to speak with him when I returned to Guatemala City.

My story was wrecked without Alfredo. In the U.S., he was called Alfred Nakatsuma. Here, he was Alfredo Nakatsuma-Vaca. He grew up in east Los Angeles, the son of a Japanese father and a Mayan-Mexican mother. When it came time for school, his parents sent him to a private Catholic academy out of the neighborhood. At the academy, he was a dirty wetback, a Mexican *chollo* gangster. Back in the neighborhood, surrounded by Mexican *chollo* gangsters, he was a slant-eyed Jap. And now here he was, in

Guatemala, still trying to walk between gangs, except this time the gangs had money and power. Some had government posts.

But now it looked like we would pass in the air somewhere over central Guatemala, he on his way back, me on my way in. I returned to the café, sipped more coffee, watched more shoppers.

With Alfredo gone, I spent the next day seeing the city by taxi. The driver was a middle-aged man, about forty, who talked about his wife. He liked his wife, he assured me, but she made him crazy sometimes. Then he segued into a political lecture. And as he gave me his lecture, he became increasingly passionate. One word began smashing into another, creating a mental traffic jam in my head. He did not like Jorge Serrano, who was then president. Serrano, the first non-Catholic to win a presidential election in Central American history, made him nervous with all his Pentacostalist evangelical talk. That reminded him of the dictator, General Ríos Montt and his bible-toting spiritual advisers from the California-based Church of the Word. They were spooky. But he liked the way things were going in the country. The civil war was all but over. The rightists, he said, had slunk back into their holes of hatred, determined to make a little money instead of spending it on guns and ammo and propping up the generals. And it was okay to say you didn't like the president.

"That is democracy, no?" It was a question seeking an answer from an American he figured was supposed to know about democracy.

I wrestled with this big question until I finally agreed that, yes, most Americans reckoned democracy to be the unfettered right to cuss out the president.

There was still too much corruption, he said. Things were difficult for honest people. But at least they had elections, now.

And that was something.

Almost from the moment of independence in 1821, Guatemala had been run by the generals and dictators. Efforts at democracy were short-lived. When the National Assembly elected a general,

Jorge Castañeda, as president in 1944, he was overthrown within the year. In 1950, Jacobo Arbenz Guzmán won elections and vowed to reform Guatemala, starting with the huge *estancias*, plantations that locked up most of the land in the hands of very few people. Arbenz expropriated private farms of over ninety hectares, gave the former owners government bonds, and redistributed the land to peasant farmers. But Arbenz underestimated the power of the banana.

About forty-five percent of all the expropriated land belonged to the U.S.-owned United Fruit Company, the single most powerful force in Central America, the company that gave the name "banana republic" to the banana republics. United Fruit and the U.S. government aided a counterrevolution that installed Colonel Carlos Castillo Armas in 1954. The peasants who had just moved in were now kicked out. The land was given back to the former owners. Castillo was shot in 1957.

From then on Guatemala simmered between the forces of right and left. The civil war heated up and cooled down. In the late 1970s the regime was paranoid and merciless. An estimated five thousand people were assassinated. Finally, a new constitution was created in 1984, though the killing did not stop. In fact, over the past three decades, one hundred thousand people or more have been killed.

When Serrano was elected in 1991, the public held its breath. But Serrano stayed in power, a while anyway, and the country had its first transfer of rule from one elected civilian to another. But then Serrano, backed by the military, launched his own coup. This time, though, the people in the city, maybe even my taxi driver, said no. They rose into the streets and forced the generals to step down. Serrano's former human rights ombudsman, Ramiro de León Carpio, was installed as president. Naturally, though, there were accusations that he was a puppet of the military, especially after early 1995, when he backed up a Guatemalan colonel who was accused of being on the CIA payroll and of ordering the killings of a Guatemalan rebel married to an American lawyer, and an American innkeeper, Michael Devine.

Devine was killed in Poptún, southern Petén.

My driver took me to a park on the far northern edge of the city. There, near the Diamante Olímpico de Béisbol, was the Mapa en Relieve, a giant concrete relief map of the country. A three-story platform rose out of the Atlantic Ocean. From there, I could see an entire concrete Guatemala. There was Guatemala City, nestled among the volcanic peaks, and Lake Atitlán and Chichicaste-nango, the tongue-twister tourist town just north of the lake. Very far away, over the hills where the roads end, was el Petén, a flat, grey mass on the cement. It looked much more like part of Belize or Mexico than of Guatemala. One narrow ligament of a road con-nected Guatemala proper to the jungle.

It looked like an easy place to ignore. Which is just about what everybody did for a very long time.

But for some reason, still unexplained, the Maya thought the jungle was a great place to build cities. So they set up shop. Over fifteen hundred years, from about 600 B.C. to about 900 A.D., the Maya in Petén built cities, farmlands, irrigation canals, reservoirs, temples, small towns, roads. Tikal, the New York of Maya civiliza-tion, had perhaps fifty thousand people and at least three thousand structures. Nobody knows how many Maya lived in the Petén at its most populous, but it was close to two million. By the time the Spanish conquistadors arrived in the 1620s, however, there was not much raping and pillaging to do in Petén. Tikal had collapsed.

The Maya that remained lived on tiny farms, hunted, and set-tled in small communities like an island in Lake Petén-Itzá they called Tayasal; later, when the Spanish moved in, it would be called Flores. And the world went on without them. Tikal was "discov-ered" in the 1800s by the then-governor of Petén, though people around Petén-Itzá always knew it was there. Archaeologists visited the city in fits and starts until 1956, when the University of Penn-sylvania undertook massive excavations.

But besides Mayan ruins, there was not much to interest Guatemala or the rest of the world in the Petén. In 1964, the mostly Maya population, called *peteneros*, could, if they had tickets, occupy about one fourth the University of Michigan's football stadium, which would seem crowded to them since Petén is a big place of about thirteen thousand square miles. The *peteneros* usually spoke Mayan dialects. Many did not even understand Spanish. Very few could have read it or written it. And they could not do very much damage to the forest.

Thirty years later, about the only thing that had not changed in el Petén was that most *peteneros* still could not read or write.

"Taxi, mister? Where you from? Miami?" The question was repeated over and over. At the airport in Santa Elena every gringo was from Miami. And every gringo was going to Tikal. One teenager snatched my duffel, threw it on his shoulders and said he would be happy to take me there. I was not going to Tikal, I told him. He didn't believe me. He smiled and said, "Yes, yes, you are going to Tikal, I can take you there."

"No, no, I am not going to Tikal. I do not want you to take me there." He put my duffel down on the concrete floor, placed his hands on his hips, and looked very puzzled.

"But," he said, "where else would you go?"

It was a natural question. Besides Tikal, there was no place to go. You didn't want to go running around the jungle on your own what with guerillas and soldiers still threatening to mix it up, and there was, of course, the wildlife—jaguar, a couple of deadly snakes, and such. You could watch TV if you had your own satellite dish, but you would probably wind up watching the Chicago Cubs on WGN like everybody else who had a dish, a twist that had turned jungle inhabitants into devotees of Harry Carey. There was always Radio Petén, an eclectic mix of Mexican ranchero music, jumpy patriotic tunes, and public service announcements.

But judging from the crowd crammed into the small airport, many people seemed to feel the plane landings were a good option.

Maybe this was because the airport was easy to reach. It had a paved road running right out front, unlike most of Petén which did not have a road at all. Maps of Guatemala divided roads into classes. There were *Carreteras Centro Americanas* or the Central American Highways. There were none of those in Petén. There were *carreteras nacionales y departmentales*, the national and state highways. There were none of those in Petén either. Petén did have one or two *carreteras pavimentadas*—paved roads—like the road from the airport to Tikal and *carreteras transitables en todo tiempos* or unpaved roads passable in all weather. In the rainy season, "passable" hinged on your vehicle. You were better off if it had four legs. In fact, most of the road mileage in Petén was *vereda vehiculos* or *vereda peatones* and most of this was *vereda peatones:* foot paths.

"Some say we need roads here," Carlos Asturias told me that night, echoing what I thought was a perfectly understandable sentiment. "But that is the worst thing we can do." This surprised me. Asturias was governor of Petén, after all, and politicians always favor roads, which mean more development, which means more jobs and the destruction of forests. But after several minutes of conversation, it dawned on me that Asturias was not a typical politician. He was a university professor, a balding, gray-haired, slightly overweight, congenial man who seemed preoccupied with staring out at the forest and the lake. Politics were an unfortunate accident. There he was, teaching his courses, when one day his acquaintence, Serrrano, decided to run for president. The next thing he knew he was governor of a really big jungle, a position that placed him a poor long jump ahead of village mayor in the governmental pantheon.

Then, as if to explain how he found himself in this uncomfortable position, he said, "We are changing from a tyrant to democracy. It is a little hard." He sighed.

He loved the jungle, he said. Though he was a sureño, a person from the south, and not a *petenero*, he had lived in the department for years. He liked it. But there were, umm, certain "realities."

"You must understand that the Petén was the only country left for farmers. People came from all over Guatemala."

With sixty percent of the land gripped by two percent of the people, the peasants had nowhere to go. By the mid-1970s, a few had begun trickling into Petén where nobody owned the land. A man could just show up, pick a spot, chop the trees, burn the stumps, plant a little corn. Voilà small farm, a milpa. The government figured out what was happening and the long-ignored Petén suddenly became a safety valve. Guatemala's leaders pushed the landless into the jungle. Campesinos poured in. The Petén population grew by about thirteen percent per year. By the early 1990s, three hundred thousand people lived there, many creating milpas out of rain forest. Pressures for land reform in the south eased. All with predictable results. In 1960, seventy-seven percent of Guatemala was covered by forest. By 1980, that figure was forty-five percent. And then things got bad. Every day an estimated 250 *sureños* staked their claim to Petén. The forest was cut at a rate of about 275 acres per day. By the year 2010, some projections said, two percent of Guatemala would have stands of dense forest. The Petén jungle would be virtually wiped out.

The peteneros, meanwhile, were a bit overwhelmed. "The people in the Petén have lost most of their culture," Asturias said. "Before, we used the Petén only to get some natural resources. The former national government logged the forest, and the people here got used to it, so they logged, too. And the cattlemen came on the roads the loggers made. The cattlemen," he sighed, "they can only see to the tip of their nose." And both the lumbermen and cattlemen knew the *narcotraficantes*, who knew the archaeological looters, who knew the rebels. The Petén was a free-for-all.

"A lot of people get rich on disorder," a western aid worker told me. "It's a good way to make a profit." The Petén was a profitable place. Here, drugs, timber, cattle, archaeology, conservation, and politics had mixed into a stagnant-water cocktail. There were deals to be made for looted artifacts, drugs that needed running, and business to do with the Mexican lumber rustlers.

In 1990, with financial incentives from US AID, the government tried to prevent some of the destruction and gain a measure of control by setting aside four million acres of Petén as the Mayan Biosphere Reserve, the RBM. Other areas, called *biotopos*, were preserved around specific species of plants or animals. Guatemala led all of Central America in protected acreage. But, Asturias said, there was too much *mordida*, the bite. Cash in the right hand could work wonders for a lumberman being hassled by CONAP, the Guatemalan version of the U.S. Park Service. The young CONAP zealots could be told to lay off. If that didn't work, well, some people in the jungle carried guns. CONAMA, the rough equivalent of the U.S. Department of Interior, was pliable enough; and DIGEBOS, the forestry service, was rumored to pass out bogus logging permits like greeting cards. Then there were the Mexicans. They came across the unpatrolled frontier, set up camps, cut trees for a week, and went back to Mexico.

Asturias thought Alfredo and Mayarema would help. "Now we are destroying everything; but we are trying to keep this jungle for all the people in the world, and we expect something from the rest of the world. We need the help of the rest of the world." That was his pitch to gringos, but his heart was not in it. He looked out at the lake and crossed his arms over his chest, almost resting them on his belly. He thought about all these forces converging on his Petén and sighed again. "I have no taste for politics," he said, smiling.

Magali introduced me to Michelle early the next morning. Magali was a Panamanian working for CARE, but was on loan from CATIE just for a portion of the Mayarema project, an effort to educate *sureños* newly arrived in Petén about the jungle. Nobody really knew Michelle's story. She had just appeared in Petén one day saying she was here to see the forest. She said she was Algerian but she was as Algerian as Charles De Gaulle. Both her parents were born in France and moved to Algeria, then back to France with Michelle in tow; but, Michelle said, referring to the Algerian war for independence from France, she was one with the Algerian people.

Just now, though, she was one with a very high cut leopard-print maillot bathing suit with a silky scarf wrapped around her small waist. She was about twenty-one, pretty, small and lean, with wide lips and big eyes, like a Petén deer. She was a nice decoration for the small patio of the hotel where we met. Magali told her who I was, why I was in Petén. Michelle seemed pleased. She grasped my hands and shook her hair back from her face and pursed her lips into a tight pout. "We will have to know each other very much better, Brian," she said.

With Alfredo gone, Magali had agreed to provide a few introductions, to chart a path through the maze of who's who in the Petén, to guide me toward people I should meet, people who might be able to explain what the largest rain forest salvation effort in the world was all about. That way, when I did meet Alfredo, I would have all the background.

At twenty-eight, Magali, a trained architect, had lived in Panamá and Florida and spoke English quite well. I liked her. She was sophisticated and pretty, yet marvelously credulous, a true believer who was excited about everything. But I could not help thinking that Magali was having a tough time adjusting to the Petén's realities.

"El Petén is just so," she paused, looking for the right word, "rustic?" But then she caught herself and regrouped. Complaining is a cardinal sin among aid workers. "But I have been lucky. I have not had dengue!"

Almost everybody else had. Flores had recently had a dengue epidemic and most of her friends had gone down with disease. Dengue, a scourge of tropical regions, is a mosquito-borne illness that wracks the body for two weeks or so before opening its fist. Frail people could die from it. A British doctor in the Virgin Islands once told me that he had never encountered dengue there until 1992. He looked it up. The symptoms included a belief that the afflicted would die or would want to die. The doctor laughed about that, he said, until he caught dengue. Because Magali was living near Tikal, not in Flores about thirty miles away, she had not been infected.

"But I will be," she said hopefully, not wanting to be left out.

"I am not afraid of dengue," Michelle piped up. "The diseases, they are the reality. That is life."

Magali told me the small army of specialists had already discovered many alternatives to forest destruction. "Why, there is a tree that can feed everyone in Petén!" The tree, called *ujuxte*—the tree of life—by the Maya, was known locally as the *ramón blanco*. Archaeological evidence indicated that the Maya used the tree for human and animal food. They made a kind of bread out of flour ground from the seeds. Mayarema was trying to convince people living in the jungle that *ramón* bread and tortillas would be better than corn-flour tortillas. Magali rattled off the nutrient content of the seeds and said that one day the peasants would be growing *ramón blanco* instead of creating milpas.

"It's a revolution!" she exclaimed. "There is even a natural birth control in the forest. Many of the women know of a tree that can be used as a birth control. They try to keep the location of these trees a secret because the men will cut them down." The Maya knew how to live in the rain forest, Magali said, and all modern man had to do was figure out how they did it. The answers were under our noses.

I had asked Arthur Demarest about this, about the irony of the Petén, how two million people could live in a place for fifteen hundred years and not wreck it while 300,000 were on target to destroy it in a few decades. Demarest, a Vanderbilt University archaeologist and the most famous of all Maya researchers, was working at Dos

Pilas, a site in the southwest corner of Petén. Part of his research was focused on agriculture. He explained that the Maya employed a web of farming techniques including some slash-and-burn, some tree crops, some small gardens, and all of them spread apart so that no one area became overused. They diversified crops. Hunting reserves were shifted to allow recovery time. The Maya rarely cut large trees. Often, terraces were used to hold precious soil to sloping ground. "Today," Demarest said, "where we were working, they were actually doing slash-and-burn across ancient terraces that were still usable. . . . The only way to live productively in Petén is to mimic the rain forest." When the Maya stopped doing that, as a result of constant warfare, their cities collapsed. Today, he said, the old ways could be used, but the problem was how to introduce them without creating political havoc. What he did not say was that the Maya had never seen television, the automobile, or cash.

Nor had they seen Christian missionaries trained in the North Carolina hills. The Petén was rotten with them. They were easy to spot, with their neat haircuts, black shoes, long polyester pants, and white shirts. They were mostly Guatemalans, but some of them could out-Christian Pat Robertson. I had sat next to one on the plane from Houston to Guatemala City. He scared me. He was so happy I worried he would float off the airplane directly into heaven. He had been saved, and he was going home to save his brothers. There was a hunger for The Word, he said, a strong hunger among the *peteneros.*

But most true bush *peteneros* adhered to a mixture of Catholicism and magic. Whenever Demarest made a move like, say, digging a well, the village shaman had to be called in. The new fundamentalists got around that belief by introducing the magic of the First World, just the opposite of what Demarest and others thought should be done.

This was especially true in the missionaries' insistence on

reenforcing the Petén's exponential birth rate, the most stubborn obstacle of all. The illiterate population was an easy target for the Catholics and the new evangelists, who preached the evils of birth control and the abomination of abortion. Magali had said that many of the women used the birth-control tree, but if they did, it was not working. Maybe the men had gotten to the trees first. After all, if you could keep your bride pregnant from adolescence to menopause, you were one *muy macho petenero.*

Maria's man was macho indeed.

She smiled when her children sprinted at me like marauding puppies as I walked down the dirt lane through her village. She stood in the doorway of her home, which was like almost every other home in every other village, a loose construction of sticks and mud with a thatched roof and a dirt floor that left most settlements looking like a collection of giant beach palapas in Acapulco. Maria's home was not divided into rooms. Homemade hammocks were strung between supporting posts. Children were strung like little toys around the house.

Maria was pregnant. "Nobody really knows how many people are in Petén," Magali had said. "The parents never officially tell anyone about a child until it is two years old in case it dies." A lot of them do. Maria's children, for instance, all six of them, were in various stages of chicken pox. None had seen a doctor. The nearest one was in Santa Elena, twenty miles away by car or truck, if you had a car or truck which nobody in this village did.

Maria invited me in, and we chatted for a few minutes about nothing in particular: the weather, the day, and what the hell was I doing walking in this heat? She wanted to know where I came from. When I said North America, her eyes gleamed.

Maria's house and family were typical. In fact, all you had to do to see a slice of Petén life was walk down a *vereda.*

Children crowded the next village, too. They ran out of their huts to see the gringo. Some invited me inside, to meet their mothers. All the men, it appeared, were in the forest tending milpas. The children, mostly under age ten, spent the day playing. They showed me several small objects they were using as toys. The toys turned out to be Mayan pottery shards and figurines. The pieces were ancient. I later asked an archaeologist about these and he explained that kids were always digging ancient Mayan artifacts out of the mud banks. They played with them until the things broke and then went looking for more, a cycle that sent the archaeologists into paroxysms. Personally, I liked the idea of the kids' playing with them rather than having them wind up on some San Francisco collector's office desk or the dark drawer of a museum basement.

Two children took me down to the lake where their grandmother, a pure Mayan woman seemingly as old as the artifacts, was doing laundry in the water. She smiled, a little confused. I said hello and asked how she was doing. Her grandchildren translated my Spanish into her indian dialect. I noticed her white blouse embroidered with colorful stitching. It was so white it glowed in the sun. She was fine, she said. It was a beautiful day.

A perfect day for shopping. The department store was located a quarter mile from the old woman's outdoor laundry. The store, owned by José, was about six feet wide by ten feet deep in a concrete block shed. José sat on a stool behind his counter while customers stood outside and peered through the big rectangle that had been cut into the building. Clients, apparently, never actually walked into the store. You pointed and José retrieved your goods.

"What's for sale, today?" I asked in Spanish.

"Señor," he said, "we have the best merchandise in Petén." From what I had seen, this may well have been true. "We have drugs, knives, food, supplies, clothing, auto parts."

"Auto parts?"

"Yes," he said, "we have a good selection of auto parts."

And, sure enough, there were several metal items that looked vaguely like auto parts hanging on the back wall. I pointed to one, a black chunk of plastic with wires hanging out of it that resembled a distributer cap from, say, a 1956 Studebaker.

"What is that?" I asked.

He went to the back of the store, pulled down the part, and returned to his stool. "This is a very good part."

"Yes, but what does it do?"

"Yes, it goes in the truck, and works very good. This is a very good part. Hard to find these." José had no idea what it was.

I disappointed him when I told him I did not own a truck, but this Stanley Marcus of the Petén was a slick salesman and knew he had me on the hook. He pointed to the box of Kellogg's Corn Flakes that could not possibly have been made within the decade; to the can of evaporated milk; to the faded pink box of disposable diapers; to the three Band-Aids that made up the medical equipment department; to the cans of Similac baby formula; to the pharmacy's lone product, a single, tiny metal container of Anacin. I settled on a stick of gum, sold individually so as not to exhaust his two-pack supply, and a rubber band. I gave him a couple of *quetzales*, about forty cents. He smiled and shook my hand. It was going to be a good day.

Farther up the dirt trail I met another man, about nineteen years old. He led an old nag burdened with two great sacks of corn and he carried a rifle over his shoulder. He looked at me warily, saw I was not armed and wore no uniform, then smiled broadly. I asked him where he was coming from with all that corn.

"My farm," he said. "I have a farm near here."

He was a *sureño*, new to the Petén. He worked the farm with two brothers. I asked where the farm was located, and he shook his head, more in apology than in refusal.

"I cannot say. It is a secret." And it was, too. Many farmers kept their plots secret so CONAP, thieves, or even other farmers could not raid their crop. Which was why he carried the gun. "For thieves and in case someone tries to take the land away or the corn," he explained. He puffed up his chest and posed for me, holding the gun out in front of his body, resting the stock

MAYAN GRANDMOTHER (PETÉN, GUATEMALA)

PETENERO CHILDREN AT HOME (PETÉN, GUATEMALA)

WATERFALL AND FOREST (DOMINICA)

VALLEY OF **D**ESOLATION (DOMINICA)

Choco Indian boy (Darién, Panamá)

A storm rises over Lago Tefé (Brazil)

CABLOCO MOTHER AND CHILD ON THE JAPURÁ RIVER (BRAZIL)

THE AMAZONIAN VARZEA DURING THE WET SEASON (MAMIRAUÁ PRESERVE, BRAZIL)

on his shoulder. It was not a very convincing show.

I stopped every few yards along the road, which was now a big crumbly path, and listened for sounds in the forest, hoping to find the farm on my own. Within a few stops, the hacking of a machete drifted out of the brush. I climbed up the bank and walked twenty yards or so into the jungle. An acre or two opened up, tilled and planted in ragged rows, with trees and shrubs lying down like they had fallen asleep where they stood. Piles of vegetation were smoldering, coaxed into stubborn embers by the attention of a shirtless middle-aged man dressed in trousers. Wet smoke hung in the air.

The ash would fertilize the hairline-thin layer of topsoil that lay on top of the limestone. But crops would sprout for only two years or so before the soil gave out. Then he would have to open more milpa, an endless treadmill.

I returned to the path and immediately ran into another José.

"Hello, gringo!" said this more elderly and very much more intoxicated José. He was astonishingly drunk, and I considered it a superhuman feat that he was not only walking but somewhat conversant. He had two small plastic bags of corn in his hands.

Where are you going with the corn?" I asked.

"To the market!" he said with greater joy than two plastic bags of corn called for.

"But that is not very much corn to take to market," I said, especially considering that the market was an entire day's walk.

"But I have lots of corn!"

"Where do you get your corn?"

He had, he said, a very big farm near here, *una finca grande.* This was a lie. There was no such thing as a big farm here. The two bags were probably going to be ground for flour in the village. He reached into one of his bags and pulled out some corn, sticking some kernels in his mouth and offering some to me. I accepted. José was dressed in brown polyester pants and an old front-button shirt on which the first button was inserted into the third hole and the last hole was held across his belly by the next-to-last button.

His shoes had never seen laces. He wore no belt. His grossly over-sized pants had slipped to a critical stage. His fly was gaping open. He began talking again, incoherently, and reached inside another bag to produce a quart bottle of clear liquor. He twisted off the cap and sucked hard before holding out the bottle for me. I declined. He insisted. I took the bottle and dramatically tipped it up to the sky and into my mouth, trying hard to take no booze at all. It was pure fire water. I burped and thanked him, clapped him on the back and wished him a good day. He sat down by the side of the road and passed out.

It was dusk by the time I got back to the hotel, and I was tired. I stood, dusty and dirty, on the patio.

"And where did you come from?" cooed a female voice in a heavy French accent.

Michelle was sunning herself again. Magali was there, too. I thought it was very nice of the hotel to let Michelle use the patio and said so. I said it was nice to see them both again. Michelle smiled and patted the chair next to her.

"We have been trying to find Michelle some work," Magali explained. "She has lost her job."

"Job?" I asked.

"With a devil!" Magali exclaimed.

At first I figured Satan had better things to do than employ young French girls; then I thought maybe Satan had a good idea there. In Michelle's case though, the devil came in the form of a middle-aged Frenchman who had run away to the rain forest to open an inn in Flores.

"I knew I should come here someday," Michelle said, pursing her lips after every sentence. "Then I met Claude in a club in Paris. We danced most of the night and then he said he wanted to have an inn here. He asked if I would come live at the inn and work for him. And he bought me the ticket, and here I am, but he wanted me to sleep with him. Can you imagine? It would spoil the purity!"

I looked at Michelle and agreed that was pretty darn shocking.

"Why did you want to come to the jungle?" I asked.

"Because it is such a spiritual place," she answered, shaking her hair and breathing in the forest.

"Why did you think it was spiritual? Have you been to many other rain forests?"

"Oh, no. I had never seen a rain forest, but I just knew. Something was calling me here. It is good for my soul."

With which Magali agreed and began talking about the spiritual powers at Tikal, the city of voices, the way one can feel the presence of the Maya at night, their ghosts walking among the ruins. Michelle said she felt drawn here by forces calling her name. But then all this trouble happened with Claude; and she had no money, and what was a girl to do? She looked at me and hunched her shoulders and giggled.

Eduardo, the hotel manager, a man who had lived his entire life in Guatemala City, where his wife and children lived, came onto the patio. He shook my hand. "I see you have met my new language instructor," he said, putting his arm around Michelle's waist. "I have decided the staff should learn French."

I had trouble sleeping that night and woke up exhausted. As a result, I was feeling a little groggy walking toward Santa Elena the next morning. The boy behind the machine gun was a pretty good stimulant. Maybe it was the kid's poker face. Maybe it was his rather annoying habit of pointing the barrel of the machine gun directly at me, following me through the sight, turning the gun slowly on its tripod from left to right as I walked in the dirt by the road that made my adrenal glands feel like a squished packet of ketchup. About fifteen years old with the look of a hardened gunslinger, he should have been playing soccer, driving his parents nuts, trying to find out what a post-adolescent girl's breasts looked like. Instead, he was guarding the Santa Elena barracks behind the barbed wire. Just in case the guerilla insurgents attacked.

As it turned out, though, the kid may not have been all that dangerous. It was rumored that some soldiers in the Santa Elena garrison had no bullets for their guns, which, if I were a soldier, would piss me off a little. I wondered how the commanders decided who got bullets. Of course, in the Petén the soldiers probably had more to fear from the snakes than the rebels. That was not always the case, but the rebellion had cooled—all the rebels in the entire country probably never amounted to more than about two thousand people anyway—and with all the moneymaking opportunities in Petén, attacking an army barracks was seriously out of the question for a smart rebel. A guerilla could get killed pulling a stunt like that. And besides, the only good reason for going to Santa Elena was to watch the dock at the tiny inn by Lake Petén-Itzá. You could usually count on a topless German tourist lying there.

As I walked across the dirt-and-stone causeway linking Santa Elena to Flores, it occured to me that nobody seemed to notice Flores was sinking. The first street, a narrow road ringing the tiny circular island, was a foot under water. On a windy day, waves lapped at the second street. Workmen on bamboo scaffolds were adding upper stories to several houses, which I thought was a pretty good idea since the first story could double as a fishing hole. For several years the water level in Petén-Itzá had been on the rise. All the new conservationists in Petén insisted it was caused by the rush of silt flowing into the lake from the denuded forest lands. The silt, they argued, plugged up drainage in the lake bottom. Nobody knew for sure, but it made a good story, and it supplied graphic proof of the dangers of deforestation. Bob knew how to make use of that. He was, after all, a professional at this sort of thing.

And he knew Alfredo, which was why I had come to talk.

Bob was a full-time conservationist. He was thirty, a tall, handsome blond man from Colorado who had been around the conservation circuit, lived in a few other countries, and worked some other projects before landing in Petén. He worked out of an office in Flores in a nice colonial-style building across the street from a cantina. The Petén was proving to be a good gig. That's why, he said, so many NGOs (Non-Governmental Organizations) wanted a piece of the pie. They all competed fiercely for good contracts, so when US AID put $235 million worth of Mayarema out for bids, there was a scramble. "It's all one big project," Bob explained, "but there are many groups working on parts of it." Bob's group, ProPetén, had come out a big winner, although that irritated a few other greens. There was IUCAN in Sweden, for example, and CATIE in Costa Rica—and WCI in New York and CI in Washington, who, by the way, had exchanged a few nasty letters over their similar names. There was even the Rodale Institute, the people who publish the alternative health magazines. "They all go to the same people for money. They are competitors, so it is a problem to get people to work together. . . . There is tremendous discoordination among groups. Fortunately, the people on the ground, the techies, all know each other from past projects so we get along okay." Here in Petén, aid workers from around the Americas had come together in a kind of rain-forest Woodstock, a big reunion of eco-warriors and social development gurus who had met in Bolivia or Ecuador or Peru, people who travelled the Third World, freelancing for NGOs, carting their Jackson Browne song collections from one tiny town to another, living in rented houses all complete with computers and maps and a local girlfriend and maid service, places where First World cash made them the biggest man in town. And at the moment there was no bigger show than the Petén.

Bob said the whole reason why you could hear strains of "Kumbaya" in the night air was a theory, two words that may or may not be valid, called sustainable development. Very few gringos in the Petén seemed to think this was an oxymoron. They felt that if *peteneros* could be shown ways to make money from the forest while still leaving that forest intact, the biodiversity would be preserved and economic growth could still take place. So they had the *peteneros* stepping up chicle tapping. Allspice was being collected and made into sachets for lingerie drawers in Minneapolis, for tea in San Diego, for lip balm in Denver. *Xate*, a ground-hugging palm, was chopped for floral arrangements and dug up for decorative potted plants. Cohune palm oil and *jaboncillo* "little soap" berries were being collected for cosmetics. All of these mini-industries, the theory said, depended on a healthy ecosystem. If *peteneros* wanted to keep making the money they were being shown how to make, they would need to keep the forest alive. It was a little Sam Walton, a little John Muir.

The theory had caused a schism among NGOs, Bob said. Some groups felt the newly protected areas should be off limits to exploitation of any kind. "It is interesting to sit here in Guatemala and watch these greens from the U.S. and Germany and Holland talk about biodiversity and preservation. We call that ecological imperialism," Bob said. "It is not realistic to just shut it down."

Bob said Alfredo was especially savvy about this political game. "Alfredo is shrewd. Look, you know where he grew up. Well, this is a big neighborhood, and you have to be able to read people quick, see hidden agendas. You have to know who you can trust." Which is why DIGEBOS was cut out of Mayarema and why some folks got a bit tetchy. "Alfredo has had problems," he said a little cryptically. "Let's just say there are some powerful people in Guatemala who would like to see him go away. Violence has been seen as a solution in this country for a long time. Some people in CONAP and the Mayarema extension agents to the local communities have been threatened. You have to watch yourself around here. This is still the Wild West. There is no law."

If Petén was the Wild West, the cantina across the street was the town saloon, and Bob and the rest of the white-hatted cowboys in Flores spent a healthy amount of time there. We sipped beers as Bob insisted that sustainable development was Petén's only hope. He credited Alfredo and a man named Jim Nations, who worked for Conservation International, the CI in the Petén Scrabble game. "It was Alfredo's brilliance in coming up with the cooperative agreement with the Guatemalans." Not that it was a tough deal for Guatemala to swallow. They were cooperating by matching US AID's funds. Guatemala was getting the matching money from the United States.

"Sometimes we sit here over beers and ask ourselves why the U.S. is supporting this," he said. "We think it is ecological refugees. If these people from the south of Guatemala do not make it in Petén, their next stop is Los Angeles." Somebody, I thought, was going to have to buy a helluva lot of sachets.

Bob liked this scene, the Petén. What was not to like? Sure, there was the dengue, which at the moment was a little rough, but Bob had already caught it anyway, and aside from that Flores was a lovely little spot. Yes, there was that flooding problem, but, for a while anyway, Flores had picturesque stone streets, nice colonial architecture, a couple of good bars that did not run out of beer, which was of critical concern since the transportation problems made regular supplies iffy.

It was just too bad not many *peteneros* could afford to live in Flores anymore. The saviors from the acronyms had driven up the rents.

Erick was one of the extension agents teaching new farming techniques. He had been threatened by guerillas when he was working in a village near the Belize border. Later, he was threatened by the army. So were the villagers, which tended to make them a little jumpy.

"It is very difficult sometimes," Erick explained.

Erick was a young Guatemalan, about twenty-four years old, tall and lanky and very serious about his job. He had been raised in the Petén, had become one of the few to receive an education, and was now part of the first full generation of Guatemalan environmentalists. Their godfather was a man named Mario Dary, rector of San Carlos University, who fought for Guatemala's first preserves. Dary was assassinated in 1981. Erick knew that could be part of the territory.

We stood under an overhang of the small house CARE had turned into offices in Santa Elena. It was pouring rain, the daily afternoon deluge. The street outside was being turned into a dozen small rivers, though two dogs in the midst of passion seemed not to notice. "The *peteneros* do not trust many people, especially if a stranger sounds educated. They do not believe the government, and they do not like the rebels. They have no one to trust."

And, since almost all were illiterate, Erick and the others used pictures to teach. Pencil drawings had been blown up into small posters mounted on an easel to tell the Petén story. One showed a *sureño* family with all their belongings piled atop a horse cart or a rickety pickup truck—a Latin American version of Okies— headed into Peten. Next, he flipped to a poster showing the jungle stuffed with smiling animals. This is what awaited the *sureños*. But the next poster showed a field of tree stumps. The posters looked remarkably like pictures in old American junior high school history books, pictures that showed brave pioneers standing in some thick Ohio forest, their axes in hand ready to cut the trees, clear the land, build a cabin, settle the country. But in those books, that was brawny progress.

As he turned the posters over on the easel, the tree stumps became a field of corn producing a good crop for the first year, and less the second year, until, finally, the *sureños* had to chop more trees, and free more land for planting. And always the crops would fail again, trapping the family in poverty.

But there was good news. Natural products could be harvested. Crops could be diversified. Sustainable fruit trees could be planted. "The people know they have a problem," he said. "They just don't know what to do."

"Yes, but does it work?" I asked.

He seemed surprised by the question and spent several moments thinking. "In some communities, yes. They now believe they can make more money by leaving the forest standing. But there are problems. Lumber companies have connections with the government. That is a big problem." In fact it was a very big problem. Estimates said nontimber harvests could boost a family's daily wage by three times, which was good news. But a good cedar or mahogany would send a *petenero's* family cash register into orbit.

"Overpopulation is also big problem," he said. Though the agents held a separate meeting with the women of each village to explain the facts of life, they had to tread lightly so the men would not become alienated from the program. The lessons were not very effective.

Erick then took me to see Teresita, the CARE director for Mayarema. I found her in her small office, walked in, and introduced myself.

"Oh yes, Magali told me you were around. What do you want?"

I looked in her twenty-seven-year-old face, a face framed by long curly black hair, a face with fair skin and brown eyes, and saw stone. I was convinced I had somehow cursed her family name.

"Just to introduce myself," I said.

"Why?"

"I'm a journalist," I said as if that explained anything.

"You are a gringo."

Well, there was no arguing that, but there are two ways to say "gringo" in Latin America. One way is merely descriptive as if to say, "You are a North American" or German or Englishman or another generic First World citizen. It is not an insult. The other version of "gringo," said with an upturned nose and a slight sneer, was also descriptive but a bit more complex. It means: "You are a lying, cheating, imperialist dog of a white male who craves the exploitation of the world's underclass, an uncultured neanderthal who could not name a single Luis Buñuel movie."

This was how Teresita said "gringo." I scrambled to think of a

Luis Buñuel movie. Instead, I said, "Well, yes. Yes I am. I am a gringo born in Ohio and you can't get much more gringo than a gringo born in Ohio." I was about to launch into song celebrating the glories of fried bologna sandwiches on white bread with mayonnaise, of Woody Hayes football, and tuna casserole, and Bud the barber who knows short-back-and-sides/longer-on-top and does it right, goddammit, when she said, "Ohio? What is Ohio?"

"California. I live in California."

She had heard of California.

"Alfredo is from California."

"Yes," I said. "Alfredo is from California."

Teresita warmed up just a little, proving once again that all one had to do in the Petén was drop Alfredo's name and people would be your friend. It was not me so much, she explained, but she just had a problem with gringos, with the United States. The United States was always meddling. The United States thought it was the boss. The United States showed up in places, threw some money around, and found a way to take more than it gave. Gringos, she said, could not be trusted.

Teresita worked for CARE Inc., a New York-based charity.

This did not stop her from thinking Guatemala should kick the Americans out. In fact, she thought the Petén should kick the Guatemalans out. Suddenly her attitude began making sense. Teresita was a revolutionary, and everybody knew you had to be tough when you were a budding revolutionary, even if you were budding for the unlikliest of causes, Petén Libre, Free Petén, a growing and dedicated separatist movement of, oh, twenty people or more who struggled to free the Petén from the shackles of Guatemalan tryanny, which, to me anyway, was akin to arguing Appalachia could be Beverly Hills if only West Virginia weren't holding it back.

For the moment, Petén Libre relied heavily on that most dreaded of insurrectionist weapons, the feared propaganda T-shirt.

José Benitez was wearing one at six the next morning when I met him near the entrance to Tikal National Park.

I had arrived at Tikal at five to see the sunrise over the ruins. Magali had told me that there was no experience like seeing first light strike the ancient temples, their towers shoving themselves up through the jungle canopy, seeming to stretch their arms with the dawn to greet the beams of day. Even given Magali's penchant for overstatement, I believed her. I still do, though that morning God stayed in bed late and pulled the cloudy covers up to his chin like a big blanket that wiped out the sun.

But even with the clouds, early morning was an epiphany. Animals in the forest are almost always more active in the moments just before and after dawn; and at Tikal, they take over the city, walking among the ruins like karmic reincarnations of the Maya surveying the works. Most often the animals could only be detected by sounds rustling through the leaves; but as I walked, I saw a blur of reflecting eyes in the path ahead. It was a jaguar, the first big cat I had ever seen in the wild, which, upon reflection, was the reason I gave myself for standing dumbfounded twenty yards from a very fast cat with very big teeth. Fortunately, it had either eaten recently or was hunting for tastier game like a tapir or deer because it took a quick look at me and loped into the trees. Howlers, monkeys whose name reflects their habit of warding off territorial intruders by bellowing long and low, had begun a chorus. They were far away from the ruins but I heard them as if they were in the trees over my head. Several pacas, large rodents that make for the best meat in Petén, scrambled through some broken structures to my left. Parrots and toucans screeched.

The temperature was already climbing as I stood waiting for José near one of the small shacks that served as an administration building. He emerged from a tiny house where he had spent the night and shook my hand warmly. He was a handsome man of about forty-five, graying at the temples, well built, and with strong features. He worked as an archaeologist and teacher at Petén's central university, CUDEP. But he knew little about the jungle, which was why we had arranged to meet here and find Don Lanzas, who promised to lead us on a hike and to show me some of the plants Alfredo and his teams might be able to exploit. José and I walked to a café, a three-sided thatched hut with a dirt floor, a wood stove, and two handmade tables. An old Mayan woman said good morning and asked if beans and tortillas would be okay. I asked for coffee, too. It was just as wonderful as the coffee back in the city.

José and I talked while we waited for the tortillas to come off the griddle. The billowing heat from the stove forced José to slip off his light jacket, revealing his Petén Libre T-shirt.

"Are you serious about Petén Libre?" I asked.

"Very serious. It is a real movement. It is time we stood up for this country."

He sketched the litany of Petén's history, told me how it had become a dumping ground for Guatemala's problems, how the rest of the nation had seen it only as a giant lumberyard or potential cattle pasture with no regard for residents. And most recently, how the government saw the Petén as a place to put landless people. It was all true, of course, but, I asked, didn't he think an independence movement was, well, a bit unrealistic?

He thought it was a ridiculous question.

We finished breakfast and walked toward the center of the administration compound when Teresita skipped out into the clearing, said a positively joyful hello to me, and wrapped her arms around José like a schoolgirl in love. Which, I discovered, is about what she was. I imagined the two of them in camouflage, standing arm in arm against superior forces, armed only with T-shirts and leaflets, leading their legions of dozens to a golden future.

Don Lanzas would not be in that throng. He was far too busy being happy to be disaffected. He jiggled his soft body toward me with a huge grin inappropriate for the ungodly hour. A machete dangled from his hand, and I suspected that more than once that machete had served some deadly purpose. Our foursome strolled over to one of the small wooden houses where two Guatemalans and a young gringo sat on the front step. Scott stood up and introduced himself to me in Spanish. I introduced myself to him in Spanish, to which he replied, "You speak English, don't you?"

Scott was a twenty-three-year-old Peace Corps worker from Westerville, Ohio, a fact that made me laugh at how small the world was. He had just been transferred from a cloud forest in the south where he had helped make new wells and a water delivery system for several villages. Now he was supposed to help with Mayarema, in the education portion of the project in Tikal. He had never been in the lowland jungle, so he was coming along, too. And soon we were off to see the wizard. In this case Oz was Tikal Oeste, Tikal West, a kind of suburb to Tikal located about seven kilometers from where we stood.

Movies paint archaeological ruins as miracle finds. Usually some native tribesman stumbles across the wreckage of an old building; and the next thing you know, white men in jodhpurs are standing over pits in the ground looking for broken pots. In fact, though, archaeological sites are often littered like McDonald's across the landcsape. In the arid valleys of northern Peru, small, medium, and large dirt mounds, called *huacas*, make the desert look like a minefield. Each and every one is an ancient adobe brick structure. Everybody knows they are there, including looters, but there are so many, archaeologists have to guess which ones might be useful for excavation.

The same is true in Petén. Not one hundred yards away from the developed ruins of Tikal, hummocks of forest rose from the ground as if the earth had burped. Under the trees and shrubs and leaves of each of these vegetative bubbles was a construction of some sort.

If you looked past the trees and squinted your eyes, you could see the vague shapes of buildings and earthworks. There were lots of people there once; and if Demarest's theories were correct, the vision of their eco-sensitive cities must taunt the legions of modern saviors.

Don Lanzas, though, was an old-timer, and to him the archaeology was just a fact of life. He knew the forest and knew he was part of it just as the Maya were. We stopped next to a giant cedar at least one hundred feet tall. The ancient Maya regarded these cedars, these *ceibas*, as holy, Lanzas said, and it was not hard to see why. It was magnificent. It was also worth a lot of money.

As we walked, we passed *xate* palms hugging the ground. *Zapotes* were spread throughout the forest. They were easy to spot. Every one had a series of diagonal slashes cut into its bark by a chicle tapper. Vines looped themselves in crazy patterns from tree to tree like downed electrical cables after a windstorm. Some projected spikes as sharp as needles.

Other vines, called *bejuco de agua*, were living banks of water. Don Lanzas stroked one with his machete, making a diagonal slice that cut the vine in half. Water began dripping out in a steady stream and into Don Lanzas' mouth. He smiled as if he had just sipped a fine single malt Scotch.

He pointed out a ground fungus, a kind of giant mushroom whose top created a weblike half-dome over the stem. Waves of the odor of human feces drifted from the ground, a smell the fungus puts out to attract flies that spread its spores. The technique was very effective. It reminded me of durian.

Leaf cutter ants were everywhere, carting their sections of leaves on their backs as they returned to their holes in the earth. There, they would use the leaves as a platform on which to grow a fungus for food. They were farmers, not so unlike the men who made small milpas for corn.

I ran into another species of ant when I grabbed a vine for balance. The ants live on and in the vine and defend it from intruders like gringos who grab them for balance. Each of the ants is a little acid factory. Within a second of releasing the vine, red, stinging welts appeared on my hand. This made Don Lanzas laugh.

"You must watch where you put your hands in the jungle," he said, chuckling, "especially around tree roots." He turned serious. "*Barba amarilla*, the fer-de-lance." The fer-de-lance—"yellow beard," called by the locals to describe the snake's lighter colored, almost yellowish jaw—was, I think, the only animal in the jungle to truly frighten Don Lanzas. The vipers were deadly, not only because of their venom but because their brown shades made them almost invisible on the detritus of the forest floor, unlike the equally deadly but brightly colored coral snakes. The ancient Maya may have been terrified, too. They often depicted the snake in art.

By the time we reached Tikal West, the sun was high and all of us needed the break. There were more mounds there, mounds out of an indiana Jones movie all covered with vines and trees and all hiding ancient buildings. I climbed one of them—which panicked Don Lanzas, who feared lurking fer-de-lance—and stood at its top. Off in the distance howler monkeys were roaring.

In all, Don Lanzas showed us about half a dozen mounds of various sizes. Each one had at least one cave hacked into it by looters looking for Mayan artifacts. I crawled into a recently carved one, a cool, damp coffin of limestone, and tried to imagine the Maya.

Scott and I chatted on the way back. He did not miss Ohio very much, he said, and liked his last post in the cloud forest better than he expected to like the jungle. In the cloud forests, rain forests at higher elevations—he saw quetzals, the regal red-breasted and green-tailed birds that live in Central American hills. He liked the people, too. Down in the jungle, he said, there was too much going on. "Everybody is stepping all over themselves down here."

Scott was not at all sure sustainable development would work. "Sometimes I think they ought to just rope the whole thing off and send everybody home," he said.

Still, he liked Central America. The experiences here were unlike anything he could have envisioned. "Everything here is really life and death. It's so intense all the time but the people are so cool about it all. It's like, 'Hey, whatever. I'll deal with it.'"

I liked Scott. He did not claim to know anything or have a single answer.

Once we were back in the Tikal ruins, I shook hands with Don Lanzas and hitched a ride in the bed of a pickup truck with some Guatemalans who were helping conduct animal population-density studies for Mayarema. When we reached the dirt lane that led to my hotel, they dropped me off and I hiked the rest of the way. It was almost dusk and I felt beat up. I was covered with bites. My hand hurt from the tiny acid drops. My clothes were stuck to my skin with sweat. The dust from the road had formed a crust on my body.

"Ooh, hello Brian," Michelle said from her throne on a patio chair. She wore her bathing suit and big round sunglasses and sipped an ice-cold juice, catching the setting sun. "You can feel the magic here. It is a very good day, no?"

"Yes," I said, "it is a very good day."

I had waited on the causeway for an hour. While I waited, the morning rush hour clunked by, not even trying to dodge the cavernous holes in the dirt. A couple of Toyota pick-ups, an ancient Land Rover, and several Volkswagen Beetles weaved their way into Santa Elena. I was still waiting at 9:30 and the locals were beginning to look me over, wondering what the hell a gringo in shorts was doing standing on the causeway for an hour. *Peteneros* are suspicious of everybody. Finally, at about 9:40, I heard a shout in English. "You are Mr. Brian?"

I looked toward the voice. It was coming from a thin, washed out woman kneeling in the bow of a motorized canoe. Johanna sputtered up to the bank of the causeway.

"Is that your first or last name?" Johanna asked. "People here mix them up all the time."

I smiled and said I'd be happy if she called me just Brian.

"I am Johanna," she said as I climbed in the canoe, "and this," she said pointing to the man whose hand was on the throttle of the outboard, "is Carlos. He does not speak English."

Johanna was not part of Mayarema. She did not work for an acronym. She did not have a computer, a maid, a budget. What she had was a former garbage dump. What she had was the only zoo in Petén, Petencito, Little Petén. Johanna did not even have a telephone, which made her very much like almost all other *peteneros* and very unlike the aid army in Flores. Teresita had insisted I talk to Johanna and arranged this meeting hoping, I think, that I could do something about the zoo that would bring in donations.

Like everything in Petén, the zoo started as an acronym, FYDEP, with a few cages for jungle animals. When the civil war entered a hot phase, the army took it over and used it as a recreation center; since it was an island, it was more secure than lounging around the barracks. The army even built a concrete water slide into the lagoon on the landward side. Later, when the army could recreate in its own compounds back at the garrison, the city took it over and used it as a garbage dump. The University of San Carlos was given the zoo in 1992. Johanna, a veterinarian and researcher, was asked to take it over. She agreed and began fighting a Sysiphitic battle.

"This is pathetic," Johanna told me when we landed on the island. "I am not happy at all I agreed to do this." No, Johanna was nothing like the brave eco-soldiers. She knew when something was a miserable pain in the ass and did not hesitate to say so. I liked her.

"When I got here, it was like a war zone," she recalled as we walked around the zoo. "We worked for a month just to get most of the garbage off the island. I asked the army and they helped me a little."

Supplies were always skimpy. On this day the equipment shed held four machetes, one wheelbarrow, a bag of nails that was almost empty and two hammers. Johanna had her choice of medical supplies as long as it was aspirin. There were no antibiotics, no tranquilizers. "I used to have some alcohol and cotton," she said, "but the men needed them at home." In fact, the half-dozen men who worked on and off for the zoo often split medical supplies with the animals. "The men need medications, too, so when I do get some, I wind up sharing it with them," which was the least she could do, she reasoned, seeing as how she had no money to pay them any more. When she did have a bottle of tranquilizers, she had no way to administer them to a jaguar, say, so she fashioned a blowpipe out of some old PVC tubing and used a syringe as a dart. "You have to have a little bit of imagination in this job," she said.

Then there was the gas problem. On the day I visited, rains had washed out a bridge from the south. The gas truck could not get to Santa Elena. She had no gas stored since she could not afford any more than a few *quetzales* worth at any one time. She had sucked some gas out of a friend's car to fuel the outboard that brought us to the island. I looked back at Carlos, who had been shaking the gas can back and forth. He was worried.

Besides the gas, Johanna's immediate problem was food. There was barely any for the animals. Normally, she fed the animals by begging at the few grocery stores of Santa Elena and Flores and at cantinas. The stores and the restaurants would give her food that was going rotten or was surplus—if, that is, she agreed to take their trash to the dump. She did this every morning. This morning, though, there was no extra food since the bridge that washed out gas deliveries had also washed out food deliveries.

And, like everything else on the lake, the island was drowning. A walking footpath through the zoo that had taken weeks to make had been wiped out. So had a couple of shacks and the boat dock. The caiman enclosure for the crocodilians that live in Petén-Itzá was inundated. She reached into the big pen where they lay half submerged and picked an egg off a nest. It was waterlogged.

At least local officials loved the zoo. The mayor of Flores loved it so much that when he threw a party, he raided the deer exhibit and served venison hors d'ouevres.

This made Johanna a little nervous about the tasty pacas. She checked the cages daily just to be sure no one had been shopping.

"This could be one of the most beautful zoos in Latin America," Johanna said as we walked up a rise and into the jungle. In fact, the zoo, which held the sixty-eight animals saved from dinner tables, was already beautiful. And if the animals could figure such a thing, they would be happy to live there. They were refugees of a sort. As *sureños* poured in and more jungle was cleared, many animals were captured by families for pets or were injured. The zoo was here to help rehabilitate them, to breed endangered species. Without the zoo, the animals the people brought to her would die. And so Johanna stayed on, hating most of her job and loving the animals.

Sometimes a biologist or another vet would come up from Guatemala City. Once in a while an American visited. A representative of the Philadelphia Zoo was at Petencito and inquired about the loan of a jaguar. Maybe a trade for a new enclosure could be arranged. One visiting vet was so overwhelmed with Johanna's struggle that he wrote a personal check for $500 on the spot.

Today, Manuel was at Petencito. Manuel, a herpetologist, was about twenty-five. Although Johanna was just a year older, Manuel looked ten years younger. For Manuel, being at Petencito was a trip to FAO Schwarz. Here in Petén, there were an awful lot of reptiles a herpetologist in the city does not see very often.

"You just have to fight so much, struggle without money," Johanna said as we sat at a hand-hewn picnic table near what she hoped would someday be the visitors' center. "It gets really, really frustrating. You know, we call this a damn beautiful country. It is so beautiful, but it is also damned."

We got up to go back to the boat, back to Flores, but as Johanna and I walked away from the table, Manuel shouted in Spanish. He was on his knees peering under the table and excitedly waving us over. He motioned for me to lift the table and, when I did, I could see what held Manuel's attention. A coral snake was coiled directly underneath. I stared wide-eyed at Johanna.

"Do you have antivenin here?"

She looked back at me, and for the first time that day she laughed and shook her head. Manuel, though, did not even wait for her answer. He snatched the back of the snake's neck and held it up proudly. Later, he would milk its venom. I thought Manuel was insane.

Calle Rojo was ankle-deep in mud late that afternoon, but it did not stop the men from going to the cantinas, the wooden-plank squatters' sheds that poured the same gut-twisting clear liquor my friend José had served me on the dirt road. When a man got liquored enough, he might shell out the few *quetzales*, maybe about two dollars, that it took to buy a woman for a few minutes of love on the fly. Maybe he would kill his buddy for no good reason. "People there do not consider it a good night unless somebody has been killed," one local told me. Calle Rojo looked the way I had always imagined an 1800s gold rush camp might look after a downpour, except nobody in Calle Rojo had struck it rich in a very long time. They knew they never would.

There was no hiding the fact I was a gringo, the only gringo within a mile of Calle Rojo, and a gringo had absolutely no business being within a mile of the place. So I ducked into one of the bars, where I hoped the darkness would give me a little cover while I listened to conversations. This was a bad idea. Beaten faces—looking to beat somebody else, sometime, somewhere, just so they would not feel so beaten themselves—stared at me. I ordered a beer.

"Norteamericano!" shouted a drunken man in my ear.

I smiled stupidly. "Sí, norteamericano."

He smiled a gummy smile back through his grizzled face and slapped my back. "Elvis Presley!" he bellowed and shook my hand.

Long live The King.

I assured him that my story was about him. About him in the Petén. I told him there was no story if he refused to talk. That a story right now might be a boost for what he was trying to accomplish. He just stood and shook his head.

"Look," I said. "Have you had dinner?" He had not eaten. "Well, why don't we get out of here, get something to eat. Have a beer. Just talk. No interview."

He agreed, at least partly so he could get out of the lobby. We walked out to the street, to his old, battered white Toyota hatchback. The doors did not work. We had to climb in through the hatch. We drove through the dark streets of the city to a small family-run restaurant he liked where, he said, they made good *albóndigas* soup.

When we arrived, the matron hugged Alfredo like a lost son. He joked with her and asked about what was tasting good just then. We each ordered a beer, some soup, and tortillas.

"I despaired of ever meeting you," I said. "It seems all you have to do in Guatemala is drop your name and doors open."

This was true. Everyone I had met in Petén knew Alfredo or knew of Alfredo, and everyone described him as "not a typical gringo." He was, they said, *muy sencillo*, which literally means candid but describes someone who is plain-spoken, does not put on airs, fits in with common people who trust him and his honesty. It is a big compliment.

"I love the people here," he said, and he meant it.

As we talked, I began to realize that Alfredo Nakatsuma might be the most tightly wound human being I had ever encountered and that there was no way he was going to loosen up after a few beers as I had hoped. I recounted how I had first become interested in the Petén, about the satellite photograph I had seen. He smiled. That picture, he said, hung on his office wall. He disagreed when I suggested it may be a totem to futility.

"It inspires me," he said. "The future does not have to be like that in Petén."

After all, had not his own family history been incredible? His father was a man who had fought with the 442nd Division, the Japanese-American division, in World War II, one of the most decorated units of the war. His mother was a Maya woman from Mexico. He grew up with the east L.A. gangs. His father worked for the post office, worked hard all his life, sent his sons to Catholic school. Alfredo had gone to Stanford, where he studied engineering, and then, attracted by theories of liberation theology in the Third World, had gone to graduate school to study development issues. It was a long road from the L.A. streets to Guatemala and just went to show you that dreams can come true.

"Is Guatemala all that different from the old neighborhood?" I asked.

He smiled. "Guess not, in some ways. In some ways they are very alike."

But, he said, his life meant something. He was thirty-three, single, overworked, underpaid, and swam laps in a pool as his only recreation. But he was helping.

We left the restaurant and climbed back in Alfredo's car. He drove me to the hotel, where the crowd had retreated into the tent to see the pop star. I offered to buy him a beer in the bar. I made a last-ditch effort at something like an interview. I asked about the dangers he faced, but he enumerated the troubles Mayarema workers had, never mentioning himself. There were the constant threats, many anonymous, from people who wanted Mayarema to fail, wanted the gringo acronyms to go home. The threats worried everybody, he said, but not a single worker had backed down and given up.

One young worker died in a jungle accident, Alfredo said. "He had a wife and two little boys." And then tears came to Alfredo's eyes.

"And what about you?"

"I keep a coiled rope tied to my bed," he said. "When they come for you in the city, they come at night."

The rope was long enough to reach the street below his bedroom window. He did not think he would ever have to use it, but, well, it was there. Just in case.

His background, his work, the jungle had all turned Alfredo into a Big Questions guy. When the television in the bar reported the resignation of a corrupt South American president, it drew Alfredo's attention. He clenched his fist and looked at me.

"That's very, very important," he said, not really smiling. "That's a critical development." Alfredo could not care less whether the Dodgers won the pennant.

"It's a big world, Alfredo," I said. "There are a lot of ways Mayarema could fail—population, politics, lots of ways. There are no good answers," I said, referring to Mayarema and maybe a little to myself.

"You have to dream," he said. "And I believe in dreams."

Alfredo looked across the table at me and asked, as if he were asking whether I knew the secret of life, "Do you understand about dreams?"

"I don't know anymore," I confessed.

"Well," he said, lifting up his glass, "Here's to dreams."

We drained our glasses and I walked him outside. It had just rained and the streets shone shiny black. He shook my hand and apologized again for backing out of the interview. I shrugged, said it was okay. He walked to his car, climbed through the back, and drove away into the city, back to his apartment with the coiled rope by his bed.

"Here's to dreams, Alfredo," I said.

PARADISE
(DOMINICA)

The large, balding man was on his second or third drink, but just sitting, quietly, at the end of the bar. He was black, so I took him for a Dominican, or, if not, maybe a St. Lucian or a Barbadan. I ordered another beer, another Jamaican Red Stripe, and kept talking to Wilmot Rolle, the hippest, jivin'est bartender on Dominica, whose thick Creole accent made his English nearly indecipherable, especially when he became excited or was building up to the punchline of a joke, which was most of the time.

Wilmot was approaching forty, but he was still thin and lean, and he had a certain manic energy that inhabited his body, making it twitch and shake and hustle, seeming to force even the most simple movements into a kind of hip-hop dance routine. He would mix a drink or pour a beer, tell a story, dish out a little scoop on the island and some of the people on it. Wilmot was a good bartender. In fact, he proudly told me, he was sent to Venezuela to study mixology. This was a good thing. It meant his Spanish was easier to understand than his English.

Wilmot was also a bullshitter. But he was a good bullshitter, not mean, not expecting anyone to really believe what he said, but the kind of bullshitter who knows he's on stage. Like a good master of ceremonies Wilmot wanted to make sure everybody got what they came to see. He provided it. And part of his routine was singing, whistling, or chanting the song "Lemon Tree," over and over and over until I began to fantasize that Wilmot was stuffed with lemons like Cool Hand Luke stuffed with eggs, the lemons overflowing his mouth, engorging his belly so he would never, ever sing "Lemon Tree" again. But the fantasy would pass and after two beers it seemed quirky again. After three, I'd sing it with him. Wilmot was a good bartender.

Wilmot said something about the people who come to Dominica when the big man looked up from his glass of frosty bluish booze and marischino cherry and smiled at me.

"You're from the States, huh?" he said in an accent that immediately gave him away as being from the East Coast.

"Yes. You?"

"Sure, New York," he said.

"I'm from California," I said. "But I like New York anyway."

This made him laugh. "You can have it. I'm thinking about leaving."

"For where?"

"For right here, pal. Right here."

I asked him what he did back in New York. He explained that he lived in Manhattan. That he found it exciting for the first few years he lived in Manhattan, but no more.

"What do you do in Manhattan?" I asked.

"Network TV. I'm a producer for ABC News."

He told me the show he helped produce, and I asked a few questions about one of the show's personalities, a woman I had maintained a secret, passionate crush on ever since I'd first seen her come into my living room. I was sure that at some point she would look through the screen at me, realize I was the only man for her, and climb on through.

"What's she like?" I asked.

"Bimbo. And bitchy, too," he said.

But she and the network and the city and late nights and the ulcers and the cab rides home had done him a favor, he said. They had made him look inside himself and at the world around him. When he looked inside himself, he knew for sure that his climb to success had not been worth it after all. Where had it brought him? He was lonely in a city of millions. His work consumed him. He made good money, but what for?

"So I spend every bit of time off I get and travel. I go places. For about five years I've been looking for someplace to drop into, build a little house, and write my novel. My own little paradise. I love this island, man. I think I've found the place."

Why he felt that way about an island few have heard of, an island that is home to some of the last oceanic rain forest on earth, was easy to see. I had caught the fever myself. In fact, what had started as a small assignment to write a short piece on island hiking, was giving me a place to once-and-for-all bury my questions, my search for meaning in the exotic.

I had been intrigued by Dominica years before, in 1983, because of a woman I saw on television, a woman whose name I had been looking for in newspapers and magazines ever since. Unlike my fantasy news personality, this woman was quite old and she stood next to Ronald Reagan, which made her look even shorter than she already was, which was pretty short, indeed. Reagan, who then happened to be president of the United States, was looking me in the eye and explaining why the U.S. was, as he spoke, invading the tiny Caribbean island nation of Grenada, which, to me, anyway, didn't seem to be posing any immediate threat to the well-protected security of the United States of America. But Reagan told me that we were invading this home of nutmeg in order to make the hemisphere safe for democracy and to protect the right of American kids to attend medical school on Caribbean islands.

While I might be in favor of both those noble goals, I worried a little. Caribbean history is full of U.S. intervention, occupation, and invasion; and I thought maybe the other nations in the basin would be just a little disturbed that the U.S. was dropping troops onto yet another island. But just when I was working myself into a lather over the specter of our unneighborliness, Ronald Reagan gestured to a tiny old black woman standing near him. She reminded me of a black Barbara Woodhouse, the eccentric British dog trainer. He introduced her as the prime minister of Dominica, a word he pronounced as doe-MIN-ika instead of doe-min-EE-ka, which is its name. Over the next twenty-four hours nearly every news report would pronounce Dominica the way Reagan did. So would I. All of which was an indication of how much anybody knew about Dominica or about Mary Eugenia Charles, its prime minister.

Prime Minister Charles strode with great dignity to the podium, her head seemingly floating just barely above it like a brown balloon, and spoke in her clipped BBC accent about the need for U.S. troops to invade. She explained that the Caribbean nations, especially the East Caribbean States, whose council she headed, were in favor of America's invading Grenada. I felt better. When she was through, I half expected her to turn to Reagan, squeal "Walkies!" and usher Reagan out of the room at a brisk pace, her tweed skirts rustling against her legs.

For the next few days, Eugenia Charles was squired around Washington, being introduced to congressmen and senators who seemed shocked to discover that Dominica was populated by people who played cricket, not béisbol, and had not produced a single quality shortstop. Once it was explained that Dominica and the Dominican Republic were two separate countries, the legislators listened. The legislators nodded. The P.M. smiled. The meetings were reported in agate type on the back pages of newspapers, and the Cubans on Grenada put down their guns, and the hemisphere was made safe for democracy, and Eugenia Charles went home, back into obscurity, out of the minds of Americans.

For Dominica, fame did not last even fifteen minutes. Which was pretty much okay with the 75,000 or so Dominicans. They were poor, but happy. They grew bananas. They listened to the radio. They travelled to the other islands to work because there sure wasn't much work on Dominica if you did not grow bananas. In fact, there was a saying that if you scratched a Barbadan or a St. Martin, you would find a Dominican.

But then people started showing up and calling the island a paradise.

That was quite a change from the day in 1493 when Columbus sailed by because he could not be bothered to make landfall. Since it was a Sunday, he offhandedly named the place for the Lord's day.

Despite its location in the Caribbean, tucked between the two French departments of Martinique and Guadeloupe with their Air France service and fresh berries flown in for hundreds of naked Europeans, Dominica was a world away. It was, said its few devotees, heaven for adventurous lovers of the outdoors, a place of unrelieved beauty. I wondered if that was true. I wondered if I could finally meet Eugenia Charles, if tiny Dominica was the jungle I had been seeking.

Getting to Dominica involved a flight aboard a small turboprop commuter that hopped islands from Puerto Rico all the way down the chain. In my case, I climbed aboard in San Juan but wouldn't make it to Dominica before nightfall. That meant I wouldn't make it to Dominica that day. Dominica's two airstrips had no lights. So my flight on Leeward Islands Air Transport, LIAT, stopped in Antigua a short while after dark.

I landed at the V. C. Byrd International Airport. This was not the airport's original name, but after the Canadian engineers who built the airport left, the prime minister, who happened to be named V. C. Byrd, renamed the facility after himself. You can do that when you are prime minister for life. Antigua is that kind of place. Outside the small, concrete-block terminal building, three or four old men, cab drivers, played dominoes in the heavy night air on a card table they had set up in the empty parking lot. They looked up at me with surprise, and it was dawning on me that nobody stops at this resort island at 9 P.M. The old men continued watching me. I watched them, expecting a scramble for the chance to drive me wherever I wanted to go. I continued standing. They continued looking. I slowly walked the few yards to their table and smiled politely. I asked if any of them drove a taxi. They all nodded their heads. I asked if maybe one them wouldn't mind exchanging their time and gasoline for my money. They thought about this proposal for a moment as if it were an incredible new economic theory.

The one old fellow who was losing stood up and scratched the gray stubble on his chin.

"Where do you want to go?" he asked.

"The Sandals resort," I answered.

A journalist pal who knew somebody at the resort had made a call and gotten me a bed for a few hours until my next flight at 6:00

the next morning. The cabbie thought for a second and said "okay," and pulled his car around to the curb. The words SHINEHEAD TAXI were painted in big block letters on the side. Shinehead and I drove off, careening into the darkness with me wondering how Shinehead International Airport might sound.

We snaked our way to the other side of the island, past half a dozen Guiness Stout signs and over enough potholes to send my liver cascading into my pelvis. V. C. Byrd apparently did not repair the roads. In twenty minutes we had reached the resort. I thanked Shinehead and asked if, just maybe, he would be willing to return at 4:15 the next morning.

"Why so early, mon?"

"I have to make a flight for Dominica at six."

"Why so early, mon?"

"Everyone has told me I must be at the airport two hours early for an international flight." This was true. Everyone from LIAT to the Antiguan customs inspector warned me over and over that if I wanted a seat on that plane, I had better be sitting in V. C. Byrd International very, very early.

"Okay, but dat's pretty early." I thanked Shinehead, picked up my bag, and bumped into a sunburned man about twenty-one years old who began laughing hysterically. He was from New Jersey. He was very drunk. He was dressed in a toga. On the beach outside, overlooking a long, curving bay, there were more young couples who were drunk and sunburned and dressed in togas. Some had their hair braided into tiny corn rows, mimicking black people, who rarely wore their hair in tiny corn rows anymore and who, in any case, did not possess snow-white skulls that created a creepy pattern when viewed from above. But then again, the snow-white skulls were partying at an all-inclusive resort—one of many that dot the Caribbean—the kind of place that encourages guests to indulge in just as much excess as their bodies will allow in what amounts to the most expensive organized frat party on earth. Everyone seemed to be having a wonderful time. I, of course, was mateless, which in a resort like this is akin to showing up at Versace's house wearing double knit Sansabelts. I went to bed and tried to mask the sounds of heavy necking on the lawn outside my window with thoughts of forests and rivers. I hoped that where I was going was the "real" Caribbean. This version scared me.

The next morning, at 4:15 on the nose, I climbed back into Shinehead's taxi driven by a young man I took to be Shinehead's son. I waved good-bye to the soon-to-be-hungover residents of Sandals.

It was still dark when we reached V. C. Byrd International. "It is pretty early, mon," said Shinehead's son. No kidding. There was not a soul in the small concrete terminal building except a few rampaging cats scrambling across the floor looking for amour. I sat down in a plastic chair near one of the two gates and watched the cats. A male tabby looked like he would remain celibate for another night. There was no way he would ever outrun the gray female he was pursuing. I thought maybe he should wear a toga and hold a rum punch. A dust ball raised by the cats floated up into the air and past a faded, framed, poster-sized photograph of Martina Navratilova. A cat screamed in that frappé of agony and ecstacy cats squeal when making kitty-love, and I smiled for the ragged tabby. The sun rose big and orange over the palm trees.

At about 5:30 the counter opened and the personnel seemed surprised to see me waiting. "Here pretty early, eh?" one said.

The LIAT plane was waiting. It was an older nineteen-seat DeHavilland Twin Otter with wing-mounted prop engines. It looked like it had seen service in some other capacity, like, say, crop dusting or dropping propaganda leaflets in Central America. This instilled a little confidence in me. I figured if any plane had that many miles on it, it had proven itself reliable and should be given the benefit of the doubt.

Ninety minutes later, three of us boarded the plane, all bound for Dominica. One young woman was named May Charles. I asked her if she was related to the prime minster. She was a cousin. "But everybody is a cousin on Dominica."

"I am going to try to see the prime minister," I said rather self-importantly.

"It should not be difficult, she is in Roseau every day," May replied, very unimpressed with me.

We talked as the sun climbed higher in the sky and the temperature of the plane began to rise. We weren't moving. It looked like the pilots had no intention of moving. An older black man in a business suit that had been worn to a shine leaned into the cockpit's open doorway and in a very dignified Caribbean voice said, "Excuse me, sir, but do you think it would be possible to leave now?" The pilot looked over his shoulder.

"We can't go yet," he said. "Something's broken."

Something's broken? What was it? An engine? A rearview mirror?

"The mechanics are working on it," the pilot said.

I looked out of my window to the tarmac below, where the mechanic, a very young man in a ripped T-shirt and gray pants stood next to the plane with his hands on his hips, shaking his head. He did this for several minutes. Eventually the "mechanic" climbed aboard the plane. I asked him what was wrong.

"We can't get the door to close properly," he said. "It's closed most of the way."

A warning light was flashing on the pilot's dash. This annoyed the pilot, it seemed, more than the fact that something might be wrong with the door.

The mechanic crouched over and walked back to the rear door of the plane, next to my seat. Indeed, the door was not completely flush against the body of the plane. The mechanic pulled out a ballpoint pen and shoved it into a small hole. He motioned to me and asked me to hold the pen there. So I sat on the floor of the plane holding a ballpoint pen into the side of the doorway while he crouched back up to the cockpit. He came back smiling.

"That did the trick," he said with a huge grin.

"The door's fixed?" I asked.

"Oh no, the door's broken, but the pen stopped the warning buzzer." He was very proud. He worked for a minute or so to find an angle that would hold the pen in place, smiled again, shook my hand and walked off the plane.

The engines roared to life, belching black smoke. The plane turned around, taxied to the end of the runway, and, like a sprinter, juiced itself into an assault on gravity by thundering down the concrete strip in a mad rush to take flight. Every bolt and rivet and panel shook and rattled in a deafening symphony. The old man up front laughed, flashed his missing teeth, and turned to me. "We get music on this flight," he said, giggling.

The real reason why Columbus never stopped at Dominica was the lack of a decent anchorage. And, from the air, the island appears as forbidding as any island anywhere. Its volcanic peaks soar precipitously out of the sea, rising into the clouds without bothering to leave behind beaches or transitional hills. It was easy to imagine Columbus, who had already visited a smorgasborg of hospitable islands in his Indies, asking himself why he should bother. So he didn't.

Hardly anybody bothered with Dominica for a very long time. The Arawak indians from Venezuela's Orinoco basin paddled their way up the Indies chain, set up shop, and started growing things. Growing things was easy there. The soil was so fertile that even today people make fences by shoving cut branches into the ground and watching them sprout leaves. The Carib indians, also from what is now Venezuela, followed on the heels of the Arawaks and displaced them, island by island, stopping only long enough to eat a few of the vanquished. When they reached Dominica, they called it Waitukubuli, "Tall Is Her Body."

The Caribs found a perfect natural fortress on Dominica, a fact that may account for why there are still a few Caribs left there today. While Europeans quickly wiped out the indian populations on the other islands, Arawak and Carib alike, replacing them with African slaves, the Caribs continued to live with some security on Dominica. With easier pickings in the sea, white sailors had little interest in assaulting a vertical island without good anchorages inhabited by fierce native warriors who ate enemies. With the defeat of the Spanish Armada in 1588, France and Britain began vying for the former Spanish possessions in the Caribbean, including Dominica. Still, few white people took the trouble to land, preferring to use Dominica as a navigational landmark during the great age of Caribbean piracy in the early 1600s.

In 1748, the French and British threw up their hands and said, "Who needs it anyway?" They agreed to allow Dominica to remain neutral and left the Caribs alone. But then came the Seven Years' War with Prussia, Austria, Russia, France, Britain, the Hapsburgs, the Stuarts, the Bourbons, treaties, intrigues, battles.

Meanwhile, the Caribs were living on Dominica, eating citrus fruits, fish, small rodents, the occasional bird, and sometimes each other. They could not know that in the 1763 version of the Treaty of Paris they had been traded like so many ducats across a bargaining table. The neighboring islands of Martinique and Guadeloupe, having been captured by Britain the year before, were given back to France. Britain was assigned Dominica.

British planters arrived, towing slaves from Africa. Cocoa, limes, and bananas did especially well; and since the slaves did all the hard work in the hilly terrain, a man could make a little money. Which was why the French tried to capture Dominica again in 1795 and once more in 1805, burning the village of Roseau, site of the only port, in the process. Meanwhile, some slaves, calling themselves Maroons, escaped into the mountains and ran a guerilla war against the planters. Finally, though, once Europe rid itself of pesky Napoleon and yet another Treaty of Paris was signed in 1815, Britain asserted total and final control over the island and put down the slave revolt. More white people came, and the Caribs, holdouts for so long against the European tide in the Americas, succumbed to disease and killings until they were outnumbered by both blacks and whites.

Eventually, the white planters figured that while they could make a little money on Dominica, they could make a helluva lot more money in Kenya or South Africa or India. Most left, including novelist Jean Rhys, author of *Wide Sargasso Sea*. Rhys, whose real name was Ellen Gwendolen Williams, was the daughter of a planter. She took off for England in 1911 at age seventeen, about the time many others were boarding boats for home, leaving the island to former Africans who spoke English to whites, Creole to each other, and thought of themselves as West Indians.

The most anonymous of Caribbean islands stayed that way for the rest of this century. It achieved self-government in 1967 and full independence in 1978. Then, in 1979, Dominica suffered its national defining moment.

They speak of it the way Americans speak of World War II as in "before the war" or "after the war." Sometimes they simply use the hurricane's name, David. When David swept through the Caribbean in September of 1979, he seemed mysteriously drawn to Dominica. He stopped there like a tourist visiting the island's natural wonders, and, like a petulant child, decided to tear them apart. By the time he finally moved on, Dominica was a pile of sticks.

"Never forget it," a man about sixty told me one day in the Roseau marketplace. "Next day you could look up into the hills and see a rat crawling on the ground. Every tree was down."

In all, about sixty thousand people were made homeless. The on-island population of Dominica was about seventy-five thousand.

The three hundred or so crystalline rivers ran mud for weeks. What little electrical generation there had been, was gone. The bananas, the nation's only significant cash crop, were utterly destroyed. Dominicans lost faith in their government's ability to rebuild after the devastation and voted in Eugenia Charles' Freedom Party. In response, the ousted P.M., Mr. Patrick John, formed an alliance out of a Marx Brothers movie.

First he promised some U.S. land developers that they could have giant chunks—about one sixth—of Dominica to turn into places where young couples wearing togas drink rum and conceive children. Then he plotted, claimed the Freedom Party, with a mercenary army—arabble, really—composed largely of Ku Klux Klan. An invasion of good old boys from the U.S. was prepared. Exactly what kind of reception they expected to get in a nation that is ninety-five percent black is an open question. Fortunately for the Klan, nothing is secret on Dominica. Gossip falls from the sky like the raindrops. The Freedom Party and the U.S. government got wind of the pickup truck exhaust and told the boys to go home. Patrick John was arrested and thrown in prison. Charles let him out in 1990.

The cliff-lined approach into Canefield Airport near Roseau felt like kite flying on a windy day. The plane bumped and rocked and presented the unappealing choice of slamming into the mountainsides or the sea. I tried to remember prayers Sister Huberta had taught me in fourth grade in case of impending death, quickies that guaranteed entrance to heaven. I could not think of one, proving my mother correct in her assertion that I would be sorry for "falling away." I looked at the other passengers. The old man was reading a newspaper. May Charles was knitting.

Outside the airport, the corrugated tin buildings of Roseau gave way to lowland forest, small housing settlements and farms so tiny they consisted of a few banana trees, a pig, and a some chickens. Lime and mango trees grew just off the side of the twisting road that climbed the hills outside town. Their branches were bowing under the weight of the fruit. The broad-leaved layers of green were interrupted only by the sudden flash of brilliant heliconia red. I had heard that a few white refugees from the outside world had arrived in Dominica, taken one look, and felt so instantly at peace that they planted roots like the cut branches used as fenceposts. This was why.

As the road climbed toward the small inn where I had arranged a room, the car passed a young man in a tattered shirt and shorts who wore no shoes. He was trying to remove his cow from the middle of the road, which was so narrow the cow completely blocked any hope of passing. The man smiled and laughed, which made me smile and laugh and fall instantly in love with Dominica. Who needed money? Why not live in the forest, pluck the fruit from the trees? Drink the water from the rivers, find a beautiful Dominican, build my little tin shack and grow a pig and a chicken?

Cool.

Soon after I arrived at the inn and met The Girlfriend, I thought I was halfway there. The inn was on a hillside overlooking downtown Roseau. A flagstone patio reached out front and hung over the hillside. A miniature swimming pool cratered the patio. An undersized tennis court seemed to float in space because it cantilevered over the cliff. Out of bounds was really, really, out of bounds, which was fine because the court had long been given over to leaves and the lizards who now warmed themselves in the early-morning sun. A tiny bar was tucked into a corner of the patio.

I checked into my room. It was plainly furnished but offered the extra amenity of fierce croaking from my toilet tank. I lifted the lid off the tank and where the Tidy-Bowl man was supposed to be sat a three-inch-long frog. The Tidy-Bowl man was suspiciously missing and the frog was smiling, so I released the amphibian back onto the fern-covered slope beside the inn. I was one with God's creatures.

The Girlfriend seemed to be getting into the spirit of the place, too. Late that afternoon, she sat on a bar stool as Wilmot mixed a drink. She was sweaty and muddy and very attractive. She wore khaki shorts, hiking boots, and a mass of blonde hair piled atop her head. A thin white man's muscle T-shirt clung to her skin.

The Girlfriend had an easy way with Wilmot and had no trouble joining in on his gossip. They knew some of the same people and it did not take long before The Girlfriend noticed me sitting sipping the most delicious grapefruit juice of my life. She asked me where I was from. I told her. We began a conversation about Dominica, about our careers. She was a pilot, she said. All this input was powerful stuff. There was the jungle, the Caribbean Sea below the hills, the fruit hanging from the trees, and now The Girlfriend, a pilot in a diaphanous T-shirt.

The Girlfriend was talkative and, I hoped, a little lonely.

"How long have you been on the island?" I asked.

"About a month," she answered.

"That seems like a long time for a vacation on Dominica."

"Oh, I'm not here on a vacation. My boyfriend and his father are here on business. I'm their corporate pilot."

Poof. There would be no woman to rescue here.

The Girlfriend sipped another one of Wilmot's concoctions and revealed that The Son and The Father, Florida-based movers and shakers, owned this little inn. In fact, she said rather conspiratorially, they had serious business dealings with the government, which, she hoped, would make The Father and The Son rich because it might take some of the heat off her, seeing as how The Father did not approve of The Son's involvement with a woman so, well, mature. And so blonde. The Father believed The Girlfriend turned the Son's mind away from business. I guessed that was probably true.

I asked what the two men were working on during this trip.

"It's pretty touchy. I shouldn't say. It's big, though."

The thought of anything "big" did not compute with Dominica. The country sold bananas to the United Kingdom, water to a few other islands, and a little lime juice from the old Rose's Lime Juice plant; and it had one or two cottage industries like an aloe vera plantation and a factory that turned coconuts into soap, some of which found its way to Donald Trump's Taj Mahal in Atlantic City. It could not even build a runway capable of landing jets, the minister of tourism told me, because there was not enough flat ground on the island.

All of this was exactly why a few intrepid First Worlders started to come. Anne Baptiste was one of the first. A former New Yorker, Baptiste dropped out of North America and into Dominica. In 1969 she began to plant a garden on the side of Morne Macaque, a low-slung mountain spackled with rivers and waterfalls. This was at a time when a few other Americans were leaving New York and Haight-Ashbury and Madison, Wisconsin, and other centers of hippiedom and arriving on Dominica with their backpacks and long hair and tie-dyed T-shirts, and trying to lock arms with their oppressed black brothers. Their black brothers on Domininca, meanwhile, thought the new arrivals were wierd. Very un-British. They did not know how to play cricket, for example, and they seemed a bit dirty. Besides, Dominicans were too busy growing bananas and earning a living to do much communing and dope smoking, and since blacks made up most of the population and ran the government they were not feeling especially oppressed. And they did not much like the pale, long-haired Americans setting up squatters' camps in the forests. They made camping illegal, a law that still stands. Eventually, most of the hippies left.

But Baptiste stayed and planted her garden. Then she and husband Cuthbert built a few rooms to rent. Their place was situated near one of the island's main natural attractions, Trafalgar Falls, and the few tourists who did come to the island appreciated having a clean room nearby. Over the years, the Baptistes' lodgings expanded to become the Papillote Wilderness Retreat. This is what her brochure said:

" . . . perched at the top of a sun-filled valley that stretches down to the sparkling blue sea . . . get up and walk out into a rainbow morning and be greeted by exotic birds, pick a banana or a papaya to start your breakfast. Dine at our exquisite outdoor restaurant in the dappled shade of breadfruit and fern trees looking out upon a garden of orchids and begonias and waterfalls while you feast on fresh-caught fish and delicious salads of natural delicacies prepared from exotic fruits and vegetables picked from the fields of the Garden of Eden. Frolic in a pure mountain river or loll in our natural flowing hot mineral pools. . . . "

Wow. And it was not even hyperbole.

Baptiste was the matron of this slice of Eden. She was a diminutive gray-haired woman dressed in Birkenstock sandals and T-shirts and loose, flowing pants and always seemed on the verge of launching into a brief metaphysical discussion. A kind of green nun. But when she spoke, Brooklyn poured out. This was crazy dissonance against the background music of patois and the sounds of bird calls. The overall effect, though, was of an eminently practical female St. Francis. Somebody who could run a business, yet scold one of her prized ducks as if it were a small child caught with a slingshot in its back pocket.

She showed me around her gardens, explaining the name of every duck, its breed, and how rare it was. Some were very rare, she said. Others, just plain old ducks. Baptiste said the birds could fly away any time they wanted too; but these ducks were smart enough to know a good thing when they saw one, and I was pretty sure none of them had any intention of packing their bags for Canada.

We strolled among the flowers and several varieties of orchids. She stopped intermittently, hushing me and my clumsy footsteps.

"Hear that?" she would say breathlessly. "Listen."

I listened.

"A green-throated carib."

For a moment I was not sure if she was referring to a person or a bird, but it was a bird, one of about fifty species of birds indigenous to the island. In fact, birders have a special interest in Dominica. The country is home to the rare Sisserou parrot. Only about thirty mating pairs are estimated to live in the Northern Forest Preserve around the slopes of Morne Diablotin. They exist nowhere else.

"Did you hear it?" she asked urgently with obvious fascination. "Oh, listen! Listen!"

I cocked my ear for the incoming bird call but was really more intrigued with Baptiste. She had lived on this patch of land since 1969 and had heard these same bird calls for decades, and yet her face had the look of a blind woman whose sight had been restored and was now being shown her first Degas.

"A ruddy quail-dove."

Baptiste walked me back into the small restaurant attached to the lodge and insisted I try a grapefruit juice. After the juice at Wilmot's bar, I did not hesitate. Baptiste's was its equal. And every moment that went by, I fell more in love with Dominica.

I finished my juice and Baptiste shook my hand heartily. Rosella was waiting for me outside. We were going to Trafalgar Falls.

Rosella was a guide I had picked up that day to show me the sights. I had already taken a liking to her. She was Dominican but had moved to the Bronx for five years, where she acquired several tatoos, a smoking habit, a hard marriage, and a raspy, tough-sounding voice. She was about twenty-seven but looked like a seventeen-year-old gang member with her battered Yankees cap and black eye liner. She thought Anne Baptiste was just a bit odd, she said—a little "natural."

I laughed. Baptiste, the native of Brooklyn, had gone organic. Rosella, the Dominican, had gone concrete jungle.

Rosella and I drove for a few minutes toward Morne Trois Pitons National Park. Green shot through my eyes and hit the back of my head. The hills, the trees, the riversides were draped in green. Green hung in the humid air. When the green curtains parted, a waterfall would blur out of a hill in a white tinsel. Sometimes the heliconia blood-stained the green, reminding me that there were other colors in nature's palette.

We stopped the car, parked off the side of the road, and began to hike. It was not a long hike, only twenty minutes or so, but we had to cross a river on the backs of rounded boulders and do a little scrambling to reach the falls. A beer bottle or two lay on the ground, signs that Trafalgar was a popular spot for the few tourists who visited the island.

Before we walked around the final giant rock between ourselves and the falls, we heard laughing and giggling and shouts in several languages.

Trafalgar Falls is not as mysteriously lovely as some of Dominica's other falls that pour out of the island's three hundred or so rivers, but it is the most unique because it runs hot and cold. One fall, originating high up a cliff, was simply a river that ran over the mountainside. The other was an underground stream that spurted from the middle of a cliff face and joined the river, leaving a sulfurous trail on the rocks and creating a natural hot shower.

The falls ended in a large pool in which tourists were swimming. There were one or two French women and a German mother and daughter. All of them were, of course, topless. Rosella was a little scandalized. Dominicans may speak a French patois but they have English morals, and naked people do not fit.

I felt compelled to hop in the pool. I sat under the hot water and the cold water and then climbed the falls to reach an upper pool that I had to myself. The sound of the others drifted away. I floated on my back, looking at the sky and the green tree tops. If one could swim in a painting by Gauguin, it might feel the same. How tempting to stay in a masterpiece.

But which masterpiece? Everywhere there seemed to be another. Maybe the Emerald Pool, a jungle waterfall that has created a, well, emerald pool. Bizarrely emerald, in fact. The trail leading to the pool was put in with foreign aid money, and, as I was to discover over the next few days, so was almost every other trail on the island, a tribute to Eugenia Charles' way with First World leaders. This trail wound through dense canopied forest. Although the trail was only a few hundred yards long, it seemed to include many of Dominica's one thousand or so vascular plant species on its twisty itinerary—African tulips, huge *gommier* trees whose sap was used by the Caribs as fuel for torches, and *richious grandis*. These trees were used by the Caribs, too. The men scraped off the bark, chopped it finely, and made a tea called Bois Bande, which, they claimed, was an excellent sexual stimulant. Sometimes an unsatisfied woman sneaked into the forest to dope her man.

The whole scene only confirmed what I was already thinking about Dominica. The Emerald Pool, a movie set in a tiny jungle clearing was unrealistically lovely, a place everyone dreams of but knows cannot possibly exist outside the mind of a dreamer.

So Peter, a dreamer, moved here.

Like Anne Baptiste, like my new friend at Wilmot's bar hoped to do, Peter escaped into the jungle, built his little grass shack—in this case the Emerald Bush Bar and Carib Lodge—and settled down. His bar was within walking distance of the Emerald Pool. He kept the beers cold with a kerosene refrigerator. There was no electricty. Guests stayed in raised shacks, Carib-style. It was simple. It was organic, and it was surrounded with the deep green of the forest. The red heliconia grew wild all over.

"I came from Basel, Switzerland," he told me. "I have been here fourteen years. Before that I was in the film and TV business. It was very pressured, so I decided to do that until I was forty and then do something very different. This," he said with a wave of his hand over the jungle and the deep red heliconia, "is the result."

"Are you happy you made the move?" I asked.

"Oh, yes. Although I used to be rich. Now all my money is in this bar." He laughed at his folly.

Peter had partial custody of his ten-year-old daughter, who spent some time back in Europe. "For Christmas, she wanted a Ken doll," Peter said, a little dismayed that a young girl might prefer a plastic doll over the wonders of nature. "She got two. With ski gear!"

Peter was a lumpy mess the way an eccentric philosophy professor might be a lumpy mess, as if he had slept in his clothes
overnight and then awakened to find himself late for class. It was
hard to imagine him running a film production. He had tied a bandana around his German shepherd's neck. His cheeks were stub-
bled with a growth of salt-and-pepper beard that was not quite a
beard. He wore old sandals. He was a quixotic character. Maybe, I
thought, he was a real-life Gauguin leaving the craziness of
Europe, the knife-throwing van Gogh.

This presented C. A. Maynard with a dilemma. The Dominican minister of tourism knew that outsiders were beginning to
catch on to Dominica, and he liked the idea. But it also worried
him. He didn't want too many quixotic characters, not a return to
the 1960s, at least. But a tourism industry had begun to spring
up. A few adventure outfitters were bringing in groups. A new
cruise-ship dock was built near Cabrits National Park on the
northwestern end of the island. So far, though, many passengers
were unimpressed. They wanted to shop. But the only things to
buy in Dominica were disposable diapers from eastern Europe,
condensed milk from Britain, polyester shirts from God-knows-
where, and local fruits and vegetables. There was not a single
Ralph Lauren Polo outlet on the whole island.

But tourism, Maynard said, was the future. "Even under the best
scenario, over the next ten years we will face new challenges." The
U.K. bought Dominican bananas, produced on small plots in
uneconomical scales, for more money than bananas would cost
from other countries. But the U.K. was now part of Europe. There
were rules about such trading arrangements. The unofficial sub-
sidy would soon stop.

"We can make it up with tourism," Maynard insisted to me as we
sat in the VIP lounge of Canefield airport one morning. Maynard
was enjoying the luxury of the VIP lounge, a small cement-block
room with a glass wall and a row of plastic chairs. He was on his way
to New York, to round up more tourists, and, he hoped, more

money to draw more tourists. He wanted 100,000 visitors soon.

"But," he said, "we are very strong on protecting the environment. With tourism we can enhance the quality of life for the people without damaging the environment."

The U.S. was helping, he said. US AID had provided money and expertise to restore part of the old Rose's Lime Juice plant as a tourist attraction. It was working on protecting the popular diving spots off Cabrits in the north and Scott's Head in the south. U.S. tax breaks for conferences held in certain Caribbean countries were enticing Maynard to call on doctors and lawyers to hold meetings on Dominica.

Then, perhaps thinking all these plans sounded contrary to what he had told me, Maynard said, "We do not want mass tourism. We are looking for a special kind of traveler who wants an unspoiled land. We are a friendly people. Our folklore is strong. God gave us a country we cannot damage easily."

Maynard may not have understood exactly what 100,000 tourists could do.

The minister also believed that the Caribs would be a wonderful tourist attraction.

I doubted that the old Carib hacking away at the inside of what was once a huge *gommier* tree could ever think of himself as a tourist attraction. The shirtless old man, rough and sinewy, with glassy eyes and long brown pants, was making a dugout canoe by the road under the shade of broad-leafed trees. Most Caribs did not make the canoes anymore. It took a long time. You had to chop the tree, start to hollow it out, burn the inside a little, and repeat the process over and over, hollowing, burning, hollowing, burning. I looked at him and smiled. He spoke no English, just the patois and some Carib. That made him one of about thirty people left on Dominica who spoke any Carib at all. None of the three thousand or so Caribs really spoke it fluently.

"It is a dead language," Francois Barrie explained. Barrie lived in the Carib reserve, in a small house overlooking the Atlantic Ocean. He had electricity, making him well off among Caribs. A young-looking forty-six with smooth brown skin devoid of even the hint of body hair, Barrie rarely wore shoes or shirts. He used to, when he was fifteen, when he began teaching in the Carib school, his job for thirty-one years. Now he grew bananas. Once, he was a Carib chief, an elected post with a five-year term.

The Caribs today, he said, owned most of the 3,700-acre reserve in common. They farmed bananas, built dugout canoes, wove baskets. Some fished. Almost all were poor, even by Dominican standards, which made them very poor indeed. Some harvested datura. Sometimes they made a tea out of the plant. The tea, Barrie said, was stronger than LSD.

Barrie looked out from his tiny living room onto the narrow road outside and into the deep green of the forest across the pavement. "Maybe twenty to fifty pure Caribs remain on Dominica," he said. "The rest are mixed with white and African blood." A woman named Ma Welch was one of the last pure Caribs, he said. She was an unofficial historian. She was trying to recapture some of the Carib language. Barrie did not think it would work.

I left Barrie and went to see Dr. Sandford, the Carib parliamentary representative and the only Carib physician—the only physician at all—in fact—in the reserve. He lived in a one-room shack made of thatch and sticks. The floor was made of wooden boards. They were nailed to the tops of six wooden logs that stood six feet off the ground. A lot of Caribs lived in these shacks usually situated in forest clearings.

Dr. Sandford was not home, his mother told me as she sat on the floor above my head. He had gone to take a bath. He was down the hill, somewhere, about half a mile away in the river. It was where everybody bathed. Even the doctor.

Later, at lunch, I told Sonya about the doctor bathing in the river. Sonya told me she used to bathe in the river, a vision that made my heart race a little. Sonya was stunning. She had skin like milk chocolate, long jet-black hair, high cheekbones, and bluish eyes that glowed. If she had hit Seventh Avenue when she was twenty, her exotic looks would have made millions on catwalks from Milan to New York. But she'd grown up on Dominica, bathing in the river.

Sonya and I talked at a small guesthouse where I had stopped for lunch. The specialties were manicou and agouti. Manicou is a kind of possum. I was not sure exactly what agouti was, but I had seen them on my hikes in the forest and they looked more appetizing than possum. Sonya recommended them. I ordered one.

"Come, then," ordered Lily, the owner and manager. I stood and followed Lily. She led me into her small backyard, to a chicken-wire pen. Inside the pen was my lunch, very much alive and cavorting with half a dozen other lunches on the hoof. Agouti, it turned out, were rodents about the size of a small rabbit, almost identical to the pacas of the Petén. "Which one would you like?"

Having never considered myself an expert on prime agouti, I was at a loss. Should they be marbled? Fat? Skinny? Did you pick them like puppies, looking for lively bouncy agoutis with no sign of fleas? "I'm not a very good judge of agouti," I said. "Why don't I leave this up to you?" Although it was my first fricasseed agouti, I think Lily picked a winner.

I spent the following day in Roseau, a tiny city of tin-roofed shacks and old stuccoed houses left over from colonial days. The Roman Catholic cathedral and the concrete government building rose above the tin. The government building, in fact, was the only formed concrete building on the island, a tribute to its financing with foreign aid money after the 1979 hurricane. It was built to withstand another.

I walked into the government building for an eleven o'clock appointment, but was there a few minutes early. I climbed the stairs past civil servants working on old manual typewriters at metal desks. There seemed to be only a few private offices. Most people worked in an ad hoc arrangement of desks and communal rooms.

One door at the top of the stairs had a seal nailed to its exterior. I stopped and asked a woman sitting at a desk outside the door if I had found the right office.

"Yes, may I help you?"

This all seemed extraordinarily low key, even for Dominica.

"Well, yes," I said. "I have an appointment with Prime Minister Charles."

"Just a moment, please."

The secretary got up and opened the door to the office. She poked her head inside.

I imagined a secretary to the president of the United States sitting outside his office, greeting a strange man off the street and announcing the stranger to the big guy himself by cracking open the Oval Office door.

The secretary looked at me, smiled, and held the door open. I walked through and completely missed Eugenia Charles. This was not easy to do. Her office was smaller than a corporate middle manager's. A breeze from an open window ruffled the mounds of paper that lay on shelves and on a small brown desk. Finally, from somewhere behind the desk I heard Charles say, "Please sit down."

There she was, her brown face cracked and wrinkled but emanating the same energy and determination I had seen years before on television. She looked all the world like a black Yankee schoolmarm. On Dominica they call Eugenia Charles *Mamaux*. Mother. And now I knew why.

She had ruled Dominica with a benevolent iron hand since 1980. She threatened to retire several times, but the people weren't sure what they would do if she did. Her parliamentary majorities were slimmer than they once had been, but even at eighty-four, *Mamaux* was still the mother of her country.

We talked about the island, about her future, about her political friends, about the time I first heard her name.

Her face brightened. "Yes, my friend Ronald. Oh, he had his fingers on everything. He wasn't as unaware as they are saying now. He knew what was going on." Ronald. And she called Thatcher "Maggie." Charles had outlasted them both.

"The last change of government here was not a very smooth transition," I said.

"No. Some crazy fools in the KKK. . . . That David Duke was one of them. . . . You know, you have an awful lot of oddballs in your country." I laughed and said that was probably true and I hoped they would not find their way to Dominica.

"Oh, God, no. We had that once, you know. Just out there squatting, smoking pot. That's not the kind of person we are looking for." That was not exactly the kind of person I had meant.

She was, she said, a defender of the environment, but a practical one. When she heard a Sisserou parrot had been smuggled into the U.K., she called "Maggie" to personally request its return. When one wound up in Canada, she said, "I called Mulrooney and told him I wanted my parrot back."

She got it back. Somehow, she got almost everything she wanted. She was shrewd. Perhaps it came from her British training as a courtroom lawyer, the career she selected and practiced for thirty years in Britain and Canada. "I loved it," she recalled. Then family heritage—her father was a legislator—and a former government she saw as oppressive steered her into her own run for office. Once there, she aligned herself with the new conservative big boys, Reagan, Thatcher, Joe Clark in Canada.

She, on the other hand, was a socialist. "In this part of the world," she said, "everybody has to be a little bit socialist."

But she also knew she was a Caribbean Blanche DuBois, depending upon the kindness of rich strangers. Just then, foreign aid did not flow to socialists.

Pragmatism carried over domestically. The island had always

been short of electricity. She squeezed out aid money for a hydro-electric power plant that forced the damming of a majestic river.

"An Englishman came to me complaining about the hydro project," she said. "I said 'What would you rather have, nuclear?' "

"Conservation is not a new idea," Charles said a little defensively. "It is a choice. Timber or trees? For two years we could not make up our minds. After the hurricane, we did lumbering because of the devastation and then we finally decided not to allow vast timbering. Now there is a little logging on the island and it is consumed domestically."

Charles became *Mamaux* when she mentioned tourism. "We do not want mass tourism. It is not good for the people to see tourists spending money easily." But, she said laughing, "We do not want any poor tourists. We want wealthy tourists, but we want them to be circumspect in how they spend." Judging from the stocks on shop shelves, that did not seem to be a problem.

It was late in the day by the time I returned to the inn from Roseau. Wilmot was behind the bar. The Girlfriend was in front of the bar. There was still no sign of The Boyfriend or The Father. A middle-aged couple from New York had checked in since my original arrival, but I had seen little of them. They were divers and spent their days on a boat or under the water, but now they were at the bar, too. It was a full house.

I asked Wilmot for a beer and a little advice. I had covered most of the island, which was not hard with a country thirty miles long by fifteen miles wide, and had been saving the premier hike for last. I had heard it was a rugged all-day trek over a ridge of mountains to the famous Boiling Lake. I considered going alone, but Arlington James, the Dominican forest ranger with the country's parks service, had told me that parts of the trail were washed out and treacherous and strongly advised going with a guide.

"Know anybody, Wilmot?"

"Know anybody? Oh, mon, you got de bez guide on de islands right here, mon!"

"You're a guide, Wilmot?" asked The Girlfriend.

"I be anyting you need."

This was pretty true. Most Dominicans had many professions, depending on the need of the person with the money. Experience level was irrelevant. If you said you needed a guide, a driver, a carpenter, all you had to do was ask the farmer, the fisherman, or the bartender and they would gladly call themselves adept at whatever profession you needed.

"Ever been to the Boiling Lake?" I asked.

"Ever been? Mon, I ben goin' dare since I was a leetle, leetle boy. I ben dare turty, forty times."

It is a Dominican tradition to take schoolchildren on the arduous hike as a kind of rite of passage and indoctrination into the wonders of their island's geography. Thirty or forty times sounded like an exaggeration, but Wilmot had undoubtedly been there at least once, which was once more than me.

We struck a deal. The divers thought it sounded like a good idea to take a day off from the sea, so they put their cash into the pot and we set an early morning departure time.

There are two classic hikes on Dominica: to the top of Morne Diablotin—situated in the northern forest preserve in the parrot habitat and the highest point on the island at 4,747 feet—and to the Boiling Lake in Morne Trois Pitons National Park. The lake is really a deep depression in a volcanic lava field. Water flows into the depression. A fumerole, a vent into the earth's innards, sits in the center of this giant pit. Hot gases pour out of the fumerole, roil the lake, and shoot the water's temperature past boiling. Nobody has measured the temperature at the lake's center directly above the vent. The lake has been plumbed to depths of about two hundred feet.

While the lake was an interesting oddity and a perfect goal for a hike, the trip was really the point. There were three types of rain forest on Dominica—lowland, montane, and elfin—and the trail to the lake would lead us, said Arlington James, through all three.

We arrived in the village of Laudat by seven in the morning, and Wilmot had already run through several complete "Lemon Trees." As we drove through the village, he pointed out his cousins' houses, his uncles' houses, his aunts' houses. Almost all the houses in Laudat were owned by Rolles.

"A long time ago, a man walk from mountain top to mountain top on dis island," Wilmot said. "His name was Rolle, and he make a lotta babies."

Laudat's elevation placed it at the end of lowland forest like that surrounding the Emerald Pool and Peter's bush bar. The van we had hired dropped us off on the outskirts of the village, and we walked up a dirt and gravel road toward the trailhead. The road passed the hydroelectric plant Charles had told me about. It was a very small project, but by Dominincan scale, it was a major construction job. And it did wreck the river. It also brought electricity to hundreds of people.

It was pretty obvious early on that this hike was going to be vertical. We crossed Titou (TeeToo) Gorge, a lava flow that split upon cooling to form a deep, steep wedge. We could hear an invisible river rushing away somewhere down there.

As lowland forest gave way to montane, a few conifers appeared and then dominated the landscape. Almost all were *wezinye montany*, the only native conifer on the island.

Other than mosquitoes, there were few animals visible from the trail, and the forest was so dense at times that venturing off the trail was out of the question. In places, the muddy path was a foot or so wide. Stepping off it meant stepping off a sheer cliff and a drop of two hundred feet. Wilmot pointed to a spot where a woman had died in a fall several months before.

Still, I kept my head down, looking for small animals. And also to avoid slipping on the wet rocks that stuck like speed bumps above the soil. An agouti ran across the trail just ahead of me. I hoped it wasn't a relative of Lily's entree.

As we walked along a brief and very welcome downslope, a hercules beetle flopped a leaf over just inches from my toe. It stopped me dead. The beetle was about seven centimeters long. At least half of that length was taken up by one tremendous black claw sticking out the front of its body where a head should have been. This was an insect out of a bad post-nuclear B-movie. Radiation had mutated its head into a giant claw and some gigantic mother was no doubt waiting over the next ridge. Apparently, the beetle uses the huge mandible to grip twigs. It then flaps its wings, spinning itself madly around and around the circumference to saw the twig off a tree. Nobody has actually seen this. I had my doubts.

Other than the birds, there wasn't much wildlife to be seen on Domininca. There were several species of bats and small lizards. The island had snakes, too, three species including the Tête chien, a boa constrictor that feeds on smaller rodents and looks much more dangerous than it is. There is even a Carib legend that a stair-caselike lava flow into the sea was created by a Tête chien. In this Eden, even the snakes were benevolent.

Wilmot did not do much guiding. Although the trail was not very well marked, the geography of the route left little choice for us, so Wilmot simply walked ahead, virtually skipping his way up the steep hillsides humming "Lemon Tree" and telling us stories from his days in Venezuela where he knew "many very famous peoples." The rest of us meanwhile, were taking more scenic-view stops than the scenery justified.

By the time we reached the top of Morne Nicholls, at an elevation of about three thousand feet, we had entered elfin woodland where the trees and shrubs were forever stunted and tilted at odd angles as a result of the sea winds that came streaking over the mountains. Here we stood astride the island's spine, the gray of the Atlantic to the east, the crystal blue of the Caribbean to the west. The clouds were about ten feet above our heads. A light mist dusted the warped trees. When we looked under the clouds, we could see a gleaming white cruise ship far off the coast.

None of us wanted to be on it.

Rains had washed out much of the trail down Morne Nicholls, which, naturally, did nothing to slow down Wilmot. I begged for a time out, using the rising sulfur odor as an excuse.

The Valley of Desolation stretched out just a hundred yards or so below us, forming a kind of bowl in the land. From our vantage point we could see the lava flows pocked with dozens of earthen vents expelling white steam with loud hisses that sounded like small jet engines. We all just stopped and stared. The acreage below us could not have been part of where we had just been, the lush tropical forests, the windy montanes.

The trail became more treacherous now, not because of the heights, but because of the fragile crust that lay just below our feet. Some areas were so thin that a person could fall through the hardened flows.

As we zigzagged across the moonscape of the valley, we noticed very little plant life. Lichens and mosses tried gamely to stay alive on the warm rocks, and small, scrawny bushes and trees hugged sloping mounds where a little soil had accumulated. But the water supply, so blue and green and crystalline everywhere else on the island, now ran in a hot, milky stew. Near vents, water burbled and sputtered, filling itself with dissolved sulfur that stained any rock it touched.

The valley had been expanding since 1880 when Dominica had its last volcanic ash eruption; and as it expanded, it poisoned everything in its path, creeping across the landscape, consuming the surrounding forest.

Wilmot carefully navigated around the noxious streams and spitting vents for another twenty minutes or so. Finally, we rounded a large rock outcropping behind which rose a cloud of steam and a roar louder than all the other vents. It was the Boiling Lake.

The lake was an amazing sight. Its water was shrouded in a sulfur fog and most of the time we could only see the edges of the shore as tiny waves of milky water lapped at the stones. Every few minutes, though, a gust of wind would clear some of the steam and reveal the lake's boiling center furiously roiling, the earth venting its spleen from a herpetic canker on the hidden away groin of Tall Is Her Body.

Wilmot broke out a little of the miracle grapefruit juice, which tasted even better when it briefly washed the taste of sulfur out of our mouths. We took pictures of each other, proof that we had made the trip. But we could stay no more than a few minutes. Wilmot's silver neck chain was already beginning to tarnish. So we looked silently at the lake and turned and began the hike back to the forest.

Just before we spotted Titou Gorge, a group of laughing school children scrambled by us wearing tennis shoes. Some were barefoot. All of them were lean and fit and skipping along the uphill trail with a spring that Wilmot still possessed. They pissed me off.

One looked at me and pointed.

"McGyver!" he said laughing.

Once in Laudat, Wilmot did his best guiding work of the day by taking us to a cousin's bar. The bar was really the front half of the cousin's house, in a big empty room, with a plywood bar held together by a few nails, and backed by an ice chest full of beer. The cousin was amused that we had arrived so muddy, so sweaty. He was amused that we had bothered to see the Boiling Lake at all.

"You came all this way from the States to see the lake?" Coming from him, it did sound pretty ridiculous.

Wilmot took us to see his own family home. We met his mother and father and half a dozen brothers, sisters, and nieces. Unlike Wilmot, who had spent much of his life behind a bar, his father had an old, leathery face, and carried the exhausted dignity that forty or fifty years of hard work in the outdoors confers on people. I liked him. He shook his head when Wilmot used Creole to say we had just come from the lake. It amused, him, too.

That night, my last on Dominica, I sat in the tiny bar at the tiny inn. Wilmot poured me a beer. The producer from New York told me about my dream woman, and the nature of fantasy suddenly seemed very fragile. I thought about the Boiling Lake and the creeping Valley of Desolation. I thought about something Sonya had said back at Lily's guesthouse when we talked of bathing in rivers. "My kids have no idea what life is really like. They turn on the tap and there is the water!" Sonya said this as if water from a tap were a miracle.

"They do not know what it is like to fetch water from the river. There have been so many changes in the last generation."

The changes did not come from tourism as *Mamaux* had feared. Cable TV snaked its way through Roseau in 1989. Within three years kids were wearing L.A. Raiders caps backwards, Reeboks unlaced, and gold chains around their necks—Crips in the Caribbean. Fuck bananas and bathing in rivers.

I sighed, and gulped some beer. Didn't Gauguin die broken, broke, and syphilitic in the jungles of the Marquesas?

The Girlfriend arrived and I felt better. I boasted about the trip to the lake. She would be leaving the next day, she said, because The Son and The Father had finished their business. All had gone well.

"Well exactly what are they doing, anyway?" I asked.

"They have really exciting plans for the island," she said, vaguely alarming me.

"Like what?"

"There's going to be this really great new golf course resort."

I laughed out loud. I laughed hard and long, and she looked at me and puzzled about what might be so funny.

"No. Seriously. I'll show you the plans." And she did. We walked to an upper office of the inn and there, on a long tabletop, lay architectural renderings of condo groupings and eighteen holes of championship golf that would be just a few minutes from the new international airport. "The Canadians are going to build the airport for them," she said. I smiled.

We walked back downstairs, and there sat an exhausted looking Son and Father. They were pale. Their white Oxford cloth shirts had their top buttons unbuttoned and their sleeves rolled up, their jackets hanging on the back of the chairs. They perspired a little, and sipped cold beers. They reminded me of an old cartoon I used to like: Augie Doggie and Doggie Daddy.

The Father did not like the idea that I had seen the plans.

"What do you do?" he asked me.

"I'm a journalist."

His suspicion rose.

"Don't worry," I said, suddenly feeling tired. "I'm not here to write about your resort."

"Well you should," The Son piped up. "It's going to be one of the best resorts in the Caribbean."

He described it to me in great detail. The luxury of it, the planning, the cost, their financing via a very famous European businessman whose name he dropped with relish.

"This is going to be just like Mustique," he said. "We're gonna have people like Mick Jagger staying here. That kind of place."

The government, he said, was giving some very favorable terms for land.

"But I thought there was not enough flat ground for a new airport," I said.

"The Canadians are going to remake some of the terrain in the North, level a hill. It's not that hard."

I returned to my barstool, to Wilmot and the TV producer from New York. I had another beer. I told the New Yorker I had been to the Carib Reserve the other day and thought it was pretty interesting.

Wilmot, ever the bartender, said he had a joke.

"You know, those Caribs, they smell so bad and they are so stupid and lazy."

This was at odds with what Barrie had told me. "So how can you tell who is a pure Carib?" I had asked Barrie.

"A pure Carib smells fresh," he explained. "The body scent cannot be removed because the hair and face give this off."

But, Barrie also reported, "there is a stigma to being Carib. Sometimes we are called names." He said the few Caribs in other places, like St. Vincent, Trinidad, and Belize, faced the same prejudice.

"The Carib people prefer the white man to the Negroes. The white people are looked at as money people. The white men send things back to us when they return to where they came from and treat us well. Black people do not want to develop anything, not invest anything. They just want to get a wife and build a nice house. . . . " According to the Dominican constitution, the Carib chief must have parliamentary representation. But the Caribs felt the chief or his representative should be in the government itself. "There is lots of neglect," Barrie said. "We do not have enough representation. Maybe we should get lawyer from the outside."

That conversation zipped across my mind as Wilmot continued. "One Carib, he climbs a coconut tree. He says to his friend, you wait here and I will shake de coconuts down. He shakes de tree and falls out. The boss man come by and see de dead Carib. And he says to de odder, how dis happen? The odder Carib climb de tree and says, 'Like dis, boss,' and jumps out!"

The New Yorker looked over his blue cocktail at Wilmot.

"You know," the producer said slowly and quietly, "where I come from, people tell those kinds of jokes about men that look like you and me. The jokes aren't very funny then, either."

Wilmot got the message. So did the New Yorker. We talked for a few more minutes before the producer went to bed.

I had another beer.

I am sitting in a conference in Montreal, Canada. The seminar I have rushed to attend is about environmentally based tourism in three countries, including Dominica. A man from India, a U.N.

expert who clearly knows nothing about environmentally based tourism, is explaining how he helped Dominica expand visitor numbers. He is a bureaucrat trained at Oxford. Or was it Harvard? Or Yale, or UCLA, or Delhi? It doesn't matter. He takes his special training and goes from country to country on the U.N. dole, plugging in his formulae. I stand and ask him about the long-proposed international airport. He has never heard of it. I walk out.

Another man, a Canadian, follows me. He is an outfitter whose company leads trips to Dominica. We talk about the man from India, then about Eugenia Charles and about the boom in his own business. I mention The Son and The Father. The Canadian laughs. "Those guys were such phonies!" They did not build their dream resort. But an Asian luxury hotel chain did. It opened in 1995. I wonder if The Girlfriend might be free.

I ask about Peter, about his Emerald Bush Bar, his haven from the pressures of producing European TV.

The outfitter looks at me. "You haven't heard?"

"No. What?"

Peter, it seems, was accused of a crime. One day, he returned from Roseau to his place in the rain forest. He realized that paradise lay someplace else. The blood, they say, dripped off the green leaves, patches of heliconia in the jungle.

FREDERICK'S OF HOLLYWOOD COMES TO CHUMBA
(PANAMA)

Luis would wave his arm right or left to help Juan, who sat with his hand on the engine throttle, steer the long piragua up the Río Sambú, one of the major rivers through Panamá's Darien jungle. Navigating the big dugout was not very easy on this river. In places, it turned into a maze of switchbacks. There were shortcuts

NOBODY GOES TO TEFÉ
(AMAZON)

My head was about to explode, so I thought maybe it would be a good idea to skip this flight. And all the rationalization in the world did not help. I told myself that I was in Brazil. Here, where partying is religion, here, in a country that actually has a national cocktail and where dancing until dawn is the way most people work out, a solid hangover should be a badge of honor. This wet-cement feeling between my shoulders, a feeling born of a night dancing to Bahian music in a Fortaleza club, was merely my way of becoming intimate with Brazilian culture.

Making such a complex rationalization stick requires more cognitive thought than I could muster. So I just remained bleary-eyed, standing there in the Fortaleza airport on my way to Manaus, the most famous, and the largest, rain-forest city in the world.

It is not a good idea to have such thoughts on your way to the most massive chunk of green on earth. The Amazon demands attention. It is the Big Casino of rain forests. It is St. Peter's. It is the Grand Canyon, the Himalayas, the Pyramids. It is nearly four thousand miles long. It drains half of South America. At its mouth at Belém, Brazil, the Amazon disgorges two thousand cubic meters of fresh water per second into the Atlantic Ocean. It has five hundred tributaries and carries more volume than any river on earth. The Amazon River flows through the greatest rain forest on the planet, a rain forest inhabited by millions of people and the densest collection of plants and animals in the world, most of which have not been scientifically studied and many of which can be very, very dangerous if you are not paying attention.

I kept telling myself to wake up and smell the humidity after I had reached Manaus, but I just sat on my thin slice of foam rubber, the mattress of my bed in the Hotel Monaco. I was trying to focus on the roaches, trying to initiate a quick game of rodeo cowboy. I threw a dental-floss lasso toward another thumbsized insect. I missed. The roaches did not seem very interested.

Life, make that LIFE, seemed to be poking its ugly head into my dank hotel room. Perhaps it was just too much *cassasa*, the Brazilian sugarcane liquor that kicks like a mule the next morning. Perhaps I was coming to understand that rain forests held no answers, no cure for my vague craving. Whatever it was, Manaus, a prelude, just the first leg of my Amazonian trip, was taking on a depressing aura.

A slimy, mossy city built on the dreams of adventurers and prof-
iteers, Manaus is still considered the wild frontier by people from
the south, from Porto Alegre, São Paulo, and Río. A government
worker told me that she was from "The South," as people from The
South say in Brazil, and that she was only in Manaus temporarily.
Her husband, in fact, was still in The South. She said this with a
hint of defensiveness as if to say, "Hey, I don't really belong in this
stinking place." The South is where the airplanes and cars and
computers are made. It's the place for jazz, for Sonia Braga movies.
Manaus, a city of over a million people, showcases the volcanic
absurdity that erupts on the fringes of civilization. That absurdity
can be either sad or funny. It depends on your mood.

I had arrived in Manaus, head intact, by jet, the long way around
from Fortaleza, a beachy resort town in eastern Ceara state. In a
straight line, a flight could last about ninety minutes. Mine was
scheduled for five hours. It was the milk run, a flight plan that
called for the plane to touch down in every town standing between
the Atlantic coast and Manaus. I carried my rapidly expanding
brain onto the plane and sat near the front of the cabin across the
aisle from two young black men carrying an enormous boom-box
cassette player and wide smiles. One was chubby, one was lean. The
chubby one wore a loose muscle T-shirt with the words "New
York" emblazoned across the front. This meant he was Brazilian.
Had to be. Nobody from New York would fly around Brazil with
a New York T-shirt advertising the fact he was a New Yorker. His
friend was dressed in jeans, a dress shirt, and loafers. A middle-
aged black man clutching a ratty valise held closed by hemp string
sat in the window seat. Another party of two men, just a little older
and clearly American, with their sculpted short haircuts and
Reebok tennis shoes, sat behind them.

We left the ground. The seat belt light switched off and the two
flight attendants left their seats by the cockpit.

"Hey, buddy," one of the smiling young men called out in
Brooklyn-accented English, "can we get a coupla Scotches here?"

So much for the T-shirt theory.

One of the attendants, a pretty woman about twenty-five years old, poured two Scotches over ice and handed them to the men. Then, figuring that, like it or not, the inflght service had begun, she started down the aisle asking passengers what they would like to drink. The two somber white Americans asked for *guaraná*, a Brazilian soft drink. Having sworn off alcohol, I had the same.

The two New Yorkers pulled out a copy of the previous day's *International Herald Tribune* and turned to the sports page. Holyfield had retired from boxing. This upset them, a little, until they read that Holyfield's net worth was somewhere just below the sultan of Brunei's. "That'll buy a hell of a lot," the portly one said to his friend. "Could you imagine what you could do with that money if you lived down here?"

"Have a goddamn good time, Gary," answered Gary's friend, whose name turned out to be Russell. Russell flopped the paper to the financial pages and began studying the bond market news. The flight attendants distributed boxed meals, the first of a long succession of boxed meals, meals served after every stop en route.

It was evident that Gary and Russell knew a little about having a goddamn good time. The moment we landed at our first stop, Gary pulled the cassette player from under his seat and slipped in a tape of Brazilian jazz. This amused the flight attendants and turned the front half of the plane into a jet-powered cocktail lounge. Gary decided to mingle. "So, hey, buddy," he said to the man in the window seat, "where you from?"

The man had no idea what to make of this question, not only because he didn't speak English, but because the question seemed so forceful, so direct. He smiled sheepishly and said nothing.

"So, hey, you here on vacation?"

The man, not knowing whether Gary had just introduced himself or threatend to deflower his daughter, just smiled and nodded and held his valise closer to his chest. "Hey, we're gonna go see the jungle, ya know? The jungle. The Amazon. Gonna see the Amazon."

The man nodded, recognizing the word *Amazon,* and said "Guiana" in an accidental response to Gary's first question.

"How's that?"

The man began speaking French. He was, it turned out, from French Guiana and was traveling to the city of Belém.

"Hey buddy, you speak English?" he asked the Guianian, who shook his head. With Russell buried in the bond market and the other man unable to understand anything other than "Amazon," Gary turned to me.

"Hey, buddy," he said, "you an American?"

"Yeah," I answered. "I'm an American."

"Cool. Where ya goin'?"

I explained that I was going to stop in Manaus for a couple of days and then take another flight to the town of Tefé, farther west up the Amazon. From there, I was going to catch a boat into the bush.

"Oh, whoa. Hey, Russell, didya hear what this guy's doin'? Man, that sounds pretty wild. We wanna do that. We're just takin' a quick trip here 'cause we always wanted to see the Amazon and we were in Brazil so we figured we oughta do it while we were here."

"Well," I said, "I've always wanted to see the Amazon, too."

Gary and Russell did not look like Amazonian adventurers. I took them for young corporate executives working in Brazil, maybe enjoying a long weekend. They were, after all, on their third Scotch, now, and I was surprised they didn't seem to show any more effects than extreme ebullience. But Gary and Rusell had become immune to booze, a trait I envied at the moment, during their time in Brazil, a time that had nothing to do with business and everything to do with fun. They were childhood buddies taking some time off for a Brazilian vacation that had turned into a roving party.

"Supposed to be here just three weeks," Gary said, sipping from his glass.

"Yeah, the three weeks were up two weeks ago," laughed Russell. "This place is just too good to leave."

The plane took off again, and the flight attendants politely asked Gary and Russell to stow their boom box.

"Have you seen the women down here?" Gary asked.

I assured him that I had, in fact, seen women.

"They're incredible. They're all over you. It's great."

This was absolutely true, but by the time I had figured this out, I was very disappointed. When I first arrived in Brazil, I met several young women who all kissed me hungrily on both my cheeks in a traditional Brazilian greeting. I, of course, attributed this to my astonishing physique, my chisled features, my seductive eyes. It was only later that I realized I do not have an astonishing physique, chisled features, or seductive eyes. But for about two days I was convinced that I had become a cross between James Bond and a rock star. At night, in clubs, over sips of *caipirinhas*, the limey national cocktail, women who had never laid eyes on me before would smile, tip back their heads, and laugh and shake their hair just so. At one packed dance club, I put my hands on the shoulder of a young woman in a microscopic white skirt to gently move her out of the way as I passed. She turned, smiled, and threw her arms around me, seductively pushing her hip into mine to initiate a dance.

I was a god to women.

Unfortunately, I soon understood, I had very little to do with any of this. It was them. Brazilian women are the friendliest women on the planet. Gary and Russell were two prospectors who had hit a vein of gold.

They had spent a week or so in the Río area. They had met women. They had gotten to know these women very well. Then they moved on, their trail watered by the tears of girls they left behind, to two other coastal cities where they rented short-term apartments and met more women. They got to know these women very well, too.

The two Americans sitting behind Gary and Russell had been listening to how the New Yorkers had left cracked hearts and satisfied, smiling, crying women scattered over the countryside. Finally, one, a blond, muscular man, spoke up.

"You've gotta watch that," he said sternly. "There's rampant gonorrhea going on down here. Their ethics aren't like ours in the States."

That, of course, was precisely why Gary and Russell were having such a good time. They smiled a little and opened a small book in which the girls of five-day passions had written intimate messages. They were in Portuguese. The girls had spoken no English, proof, I assumed, that lust, like love, knows no language barrier.

But since neither Gary nor Russell could read a word, they were stymied and still eager to find out what their paramours had written.

"I speak Portuguese," said the blond man, who I later learned was named Denny. Gary and Russell passed the book back to Denny and cocked their ears. Half a dozen women had written short love poems. One wrote of her disappointment that the two wanderers would be carried away on the giant silver wings of an airplane and said she had always wanted to see America. "Of course, that's what they all want, you know," Denny said, looking up from the page. "These girls just want to get to the States."

Denny, it seemed, wasn't much of a romantic. What he was, was a pastor in the Seventh-Day Adventist church. He flies down to Brazil in an annual pilgrimmage to lead a medical team up and down the Amazon. He and his team visit villages from Manaus east toward the Atlantic, dispensing a little medicine and a lot of God. He was born in the Amazon, the son of missionaries like himself, and you could tell he didn't like the idea of a couple of young yahoos running around in his jungle wreaking havoc with the sexual ethics of the locals, undoing the good he was trying to do by preparing the natives for Christ's imminent arrival. So he decided to protect the virtue of the Amazonian girls by telling Gary and Russell what to expect in the rain forest.

By our third stop, Denny had managed to scare the bejesus out of them. They stopped drinking Scotch. They forgot to pull out the boom box when we landed. They turned away the fourth boxed meal we were offered.

"So it's really that easy to catch malaria?" Gary asked.

"Oh yeah, you gotta watch yourself," Denny replied gravely. "You've taken your antimalaria pills, haven't you?"

Of course, Gary and Russell had taken only alcohol-based medication since they had arrived. This worried Denny. He knitted his forehead into knots of concern.

"Oh, man. Well, it's too late now, anyway; you have to start them before you even leave the States. I'd use lots of repellent if I were you. What about cholera vaccines?"

This conversation was working where the talk of sexually transmitted diseases could not, and Denny knew it. Cholera, he said was epidemic. Malaria was everywhere. Not to mention amoebic dysentery and the candiru, the tiny fish that will swim up your penis and build up a crescendo of horrible havoc until you die; and you got your piranha, of course. Gotta watch for those. Shoot, you could get really, really sick just stepping off this airplane.

Denny's companion, a software engineer from northern California who was not a member of the church but tagged along for the adventure of it, reached over the seat and handed Gary and Russell two small white pills.

"They're antidiarreahals," he said. "They could save your life."

"Wow," Gary said. "Hey man, thanks a lot."

Russell was now worried about me. "You take malaria pills before you left?" he asked.

"Well, no," I said. I almost started to explain that sometimes malaria pills had side effects that could wreck a trip and that in places of low population density, malaria, though present, is not a serious problem. Instead, I said, "I think it's a good gamble."

"So you think we're gonna be okay?" Gary asked.

"If I were you, I'd worry more about catching something in bed." They laughed. I was serious. At the rate they were going, statistics were going to catch them. This seemed to appease pastor Denny a little. He sank back in his seat and asked me where, exactly, I was going.

"Tefé," I answered.

"Tefé? Nobody goes to Tefé."

I assured him that—honest—some people had gone to Tefé, and I was assigned to write a story on what they were doing there. Denny asked me a couple of questions and we talked a little. He seemed like a nice fellow, but I wondered how he managed to convince the people living in the Amazon that the second coming of Christ was at hand while at the same time he passed out drugs to, theoretically, lengthen their lives. "Christ is on his way," I imagined him preaching, "and you had better be in good health." Did he tell them that Adventists had been announcing Christ's arrival for about 150 years? Probably not, since the locals tend to think in terms of today and tomorrow and yesterday. He was no doubt doing some good in the Amazon, which really does have a cholera problem, for instance, but this link between medical care and God, anybody's version of God, struck me as unsavory blackmail. What did the Catholics say? Or the Baptists? I hoped the locals were taking it all in, all the medical care, all the education the white people from America and Britain and Germany had to offer. I hoped they thanked these visitors very much. I hoped they walked back into the forest, a little better fed, a little healthier, a little more educated, and shed the reject polyester pants that left them looking vaguely like some New York City cab driver named Tony. I hoped they began talking to the trees and the animals about these crazy gringo beliefs.

Pastor Denny's friend motioned to the stewardess who walked up the aisle. "I'd like a Scotch, please," he said quietly. I think he was a little jealous of Gary and Russell. I know I was.

By the time the plane landed in Manaus, we had all consumed more boxed meals than the normal human eats in half a lifetime, Gary and Russell were daydreaming about the jungle, and Denny was trying to figure a way to slam the kibosh onto their hopes for a jungle trip that would make *Penthouse Forum* blush. We all walked off the plane together and into the most modern-looking airport in Brazil. This disappointed Gary and Russell. There was a boarding ramp, for crying out loud, and electronic signs, and look at that luggage carousel!

"Looks like New York," Russell said.

If this was the jungle, they thought, they should have just stayed in babeville. The airport should be draped in camouflage, maybe, or be made of bamboo poles and thatched roofing.

Lots of tourists arriving in Manaus feel this way. All the florid prose describing the dark jungle, the mystical rain forest where natives hold some sort of secret New Age powers, has done its work. The words deliver the paying customers, though—scores of them every day who take short riverboat cruises or afternoon jungle walks and buy a few mass-produced genuine indian artifacts.

This tends to turn the area around Manaus into a huge imitation of the jungle boat ride at Disneyland. I was a little disappointed myself at the airport, at the posters by the luggage carousel promoting jungle excursions and pitching monkeys the way Sea World pitches Shamu. I wondered about the purity of the experience. On the other hand, I personally consider air-conditioning a gift from God. The fact is, trudging around in rain forests can be miserable, so if a little modernization has been installed to make people feel a little more comfortable, I could buy it. After all, every tourist who flies in and touches a few trees and hears a howler monkey in the distance may be one more person who cares about whether the trees stand and monkeys howl into the future. If it took a little McJungle to achieve that, I concluded, it was worth the price.

"Hey, buddy," Gary said, talking to me as we waited for our bags to slide down the carousel, "Russell and I have been talking." I knew what was coming. "And we were wondering if you'd mind having us tag along."

I imagined these two in the forest and smiled. I liked them. I liked their enthusiasm. I wanted them to have a good time and I knew the jungle was not the minefield of catastrophe Denny had made it out to be, but I also knew they would not have a good time with me. Their outdoor gear consisted of swim trunks and thongs. "I'm not going where tourists go at all, and I'm meeting up with some scientists. We will be living in a floating house in a flooded forest. It might be a little uncomfortable."

This was all they needed to hear.

"Oh, man, that sounds great!" Gary said. I shrugged my shoulders. Maybe it would be a kick having them join me. Maybe they could shake me out of the crummy mood that had hung over me since Fortaleza. And after years of traveling mostly alone, maybe I wanted the company.

I explained my flight schedule. They had to make the same flight or forget it, I said, and getting back to Manaus might be a problem. They'd have to be willing to stay flexible. They agreed to think about it during their stay at the Hotel Tropical, the luxury tourist hotel at the edge of Manaus on the Río Negro. We exchanged numbers. Mine was for the Hotel Monaco. I gave them about an hour of sipping cocktails at the Tropical before they decided that flying off into a flooded forest wasn't such a good idea.

I had to wonder about that myself. My dark mood matched the slate black of the night sky. It was about 10 P.M., and as the shuttle van drove me into Manaus, things took on an American cast. The main road from the airport leads past the *zona franca*, a duty-free zone established to encourage foreign manufacturers to set up factories in the city—a big sign told me where that was. When they do, they are allowed to import parts free of duty and export finished goods without taxation. The plan has worked. Today, more than a dozen factories owned by firms like Xerox are located here, employing hundreds of Brazilians in a region that suffers chronic high unemployment and crushing poverty. Just beyond the *zona franca* is the new Amazonas Shopping Center, a giant, brightly lit indoor mall with movie theaters and a big striped parking lot.

By the time the van reached the city center, Manaus was beginning to look a little more the way a city in the middle of a rain forest is supposed to look. Everything was cracked. Everything shone with an emerald patina, a statement by the forest that the buildings were just borrowing the land. From what I could see through the windows, the mossiness of the place made the downtown appear to be partially reclaimed by the Amazon, and I wondered what the colonial barons would have thought had they seen their grand houses divided into tiny apartments with laundry hanging out of every available window.

The Hotel Monaco was no exception. Whoever built it, sometime in the 1970s, I guessed, tried valiantly to make it modern looking and succeeded only in creating an imitation-pasteurized-hotel-product that apparently quickly succumbed to the forces of the tropics. It was one of those lodgings where you fear for the life of the porter as he pops veins, strains against his faded red uniform jacket, and throws every one of his seventy-odd years into the task of picking up your bag. Gilberto was relieved when I volunteered to carry the bag for him. I was sure he had not actually carried a bag in a decade or so and may have been quite put out had I not shouldered my duffel. When we arrived at the room after ascending a few floors in an elevator no decent son would allow his mother to ride in, he swept his arm grandly to indicate the glories of the clacking air conditioner, the dribbling shower, the twenty-watt lightbulb, and the torn curtains. And look, a television! No knobs, but a television!

Gilberto inspected my tip suspiciously and wished me a good night, and left me sitting on the edge of my foam rubber mattress playing Larry Mahan to roachy broncos. I had tried TV. Two

stations came beaming into my room from outer space. One featured soccer. It is a law in Brazil that at least one television channel must be broadcasting a soccer game at any given moment. The
other was a celebrity interview show that, I think, sent a roving
reporter to Río nightclubs to see who was about. I debated whether
or not to stick with the soccer. After the game, the TV promo
promised, the channel would broadcast *Sexy Time*. I had seen *Sexy
Time* already. I was innocently switching channels in a hotel room
in Río on the night of my arrival in Brazil when I chanced upon
two very flexible women in an elevator wearing astonishingly short
black leather miniskirts and heels so high they required pitons and
carabiners to climb into them. They had, apparently, forgotten
their panties. Soccer or *Sexy Time*? I thought this was a reasonable
metaphor for Brazil. I had already seen soccer.

But here in Manaus I opted to skip the hope of catching *Sexy
Time*. I was not in the mood. Instead, I watched the Río reporter
snake up to apparently famous people and ask them questions
about what cocktail they were drinking and what their latest projects were. Imagine a kind of mobile Jay Leno. Suddenly, the face
of Bo Derek appeared on the screen. I had seen her two weeks earlier in the Los Angeles International Airport. We were both boarding the same flight to Brazil, different sections. And now here she
was being Bo Derek in Río. I was in Manaus. We were still in different sections.

What, the interviewer asked Bo, are you working on now?

"Well," she began, "I have a few projects in the planning stages,
in development. . . . "

Thankfully for Bo, the reporter did not ask for specifics. Instead
he launched into a give and take on the state of American film
today. Bo began to answer.

It occured to me that this created an odd picture—me in a broken-down hotel in a broken-down city in the middle of a jungle,
playing with Amazonian arthropods, with the biggest rain forest
in the world out my dirty window, and all of it playing to a Bo

Derrick soundtrack. How'd this happen? I wondered. Is this where my childhood cravings had brought me? What string of forces set into motion days, weeks, decades, centuries ago conspired to dump me at this Kafkaesque intersection? Descartes believed God had created the universe to operate like a clock—God as a kind of Swiss watchmaker in lederhosen. If so, I decided, His clock was a little off.

In that case, I reckoned, I had better go to sleep.

There is a kind of heat to the Amazon such as I have never felt before, even in other tropical forest areas. Heat there is a tangible thing, a blanket that wraps you up from the moment you step out of any building. This is especially true in cities that have been deprived of canopy shade. Aside from a central square with a few trees guarding the perimeter, central Manaus has very little shade.

So I began sweating big drops from the moment I started walking toward the harbor. That overwhelming feeling of smothering heat must have made the early land barons reconsider their choice of profit-making adventures. But there was big money to be made in the Amazon, they reasoned; and since few men had the audacity to deliberately move themselves into so forbidding a place as a jungle, there wasn't much competition. And the natives could be used as slaves. If they got a bit uppity, you could shoot them. A laissez-faire paradise.

In fact, the government was very happy to see the gold-seekers loading their boats at Belém and heading upriver. Brazil is a huge country and much of it rests in the basin. In the mid-1800s, there were many more indians than Europeans, and borders were nebulous constructs on maps that changed depending on who drew them. The more people and industry that could be brought into the forest, the more control the government could have over a giant clump of its property. Development, any development, was greeted with huzzahs. That's still true today. Brazil, in fact, still fears losing control of the river.

Never mind that some of the development schemes were

crazy—the famous Manaus opera house as a cultural haven, for instance—because enough of them were sure bets. At least that's what the promoters thought. The Ford Motor Company sailed into Manaus and, echoing the Kennecott Copper Corporation, which founded towns named after itself in the U.S., started a series of plantations called Fordlandia to produce rubber. Millions were sunk into the Amazonian soil. Rubber prices collapsed. Over nine million dollars was lost.

Others arrived on the shores of the great rivers to work the soil for gold and gems. Even today, when word of a new strike in some unheard-of part of the forest leaks out to bigger towns, hordes of wildcat prospectors swarm into the site and start punching muddy holes into the ground, sloshing poisons like mercury into the rivers, battling each other, and sometimes slaughtering indians who stand in the way. In early 1994, soon before I arrived in Manaus, miners had done just that, killing over one hundred indians in a mass murder. (While in Río, I asked Hans Stern, the eighty-something patriarch of the H. Stern jewelry empire, about mining in the Amazon. He replied proudly that the jungle remains one of the firm's best mining opportunities, and he hoped to expand operations there.) These miners are defeated by heat, by bugs, by disease. But mostly they are defeated by luck. One man with a shovel, what most of these mining operations amount to, stands little chance of finding his fortune in the forest.

But the wildcat attitude still pervades the city. Everybody wants to make a lot of money here and everybody wants to get the hell out. This is what one does in Manaus, in the Amazon. You come, you suffer, you make money, then you head to the south and sip *caipirinhas* in an Ipanema bar. But that's a fantasy for most, too, and it turns the city into an urban Rick's American Café, a place people would escape from if only they could con a ticket for the Lisbon plane.

You can see it and hear it as you walk the alleyways and side streets, which have been turned into a pedestrian mall. Anything that can be sold is sold. But like the Hotel Monaco, everything is Velveeta. There are entire stores seemingly dedicated to advancing the state of women's cotton underwear in very large sizes. At least a dozen stores sell nothing but televisions and stereos bearing names that have no basis in reality. A few stores specialize in bizarre sportswear with slogans like "San Francisco 49ers World Champion Basketball" or "New York Bulls Pro Tough." The Hawaii Nightclub vies for space on the street with Pop's Hamburgeurs. In Manaus, the First World comes through the television, but the picture is garbled and you can't change the tuning.

The port, though, is one part of Manaus that could still serve as a backdrop for the Manaus of a hundred years ago. The concrete and rebar dock is crumbling. The wharfs are gorged with boats of all descriptions from huge cargo vessels declaring home ports like Stockholm to canoes unloading a few stalks of bananas. Mostly, though, the docks are crowded by riverboats, the primary means of transportation in the basin.

These boats look much like ones Mark Twain may have seen during his life on the Mississippi. They are wooden two-story affairs painted red and white and blue and black, any kind of garish color the owners have around. Most use diesel engines that are seriously underpowered. The result is a slow-moving vessel that runs on high-test hope and a mosiac of found objects that make the engines look like a modern-art construction. The decks of the boats are flat and lined by railings with balusters. The pilothouses are placed far forward, just a few feet from the bow. Most passenger boats are about fifty feet long, but many private boats can be as small as fifteen feet. All of them, passenger or private, sit very low on the water line. That's not usually a problem, because the Amazon and its sister rivers are often glassy flat. But, when the afternoon storm clouds roll in, the river can suddenly roil. Spray washes over the lower deck. Sometimes the boats sink.

I was scheduled to take a riverboat up the Negro to a tourist lodge called Ariau. It is a relatively famous place, one of several lodges built in the forest where tourists can stay for a few nights in the jungle with some degree of comfort. But finding the boat proved to be difficult. There were dozens jammed into the harbor docks. I asked a few boatmen how to find the boat I was supposed to be on. They all pointed across the wharf, a gesture that took in several dozen boats. I slowly narrowed down the possibilities by starting at the edge of a dock, climbing onto a boat, saying *bom día* to a crewman, and asking for directions. In the end, I had to jump onto a series of boats and work my way across the port to a big green riverboat. Nobody seemed to mind.

I stepped onto the *Ariau,* finally, and was greeted by Kika, a plump young woman with a pretty face and curly black hair. She was a guide at Ariau, she explained in heavily broken English. She smiled sweetly and kissed me on both cheeks. She wanted to know how old I was. She wanted to know if I had a wife. She wanted to know how come a man my age did not have a wife. And by the way, was I free when I returned to Manaus?

Gary and Russell were no doubt having a wonderful time.

It takes three hours of motoring against the current of the Negro to reach Ariau, but it was an instructive three hours. The Negro has high banks in this area that can be deceiving because the hillsides seem heavily forested. But when the steep riversides dip lower, it is possible to see wide swaths of cultivated land cleared by slash-and-burn. Much of the forest has been turned into cattle pastures, tapioca farms, and charcoal factories. The farmers live in tiny shacks, almost always located close to the river. They are simple wood-plank structures weathered gray by rain and sun. Most sit on stilts a few feet off the ground.

The Negro itself resembles a river of cola. As the name implies, it is a black-water river. Starting from its highland source, it leaches tannins from leaves and other organic detritus so that by the time it reaches the lowlands, it runs a deep mahogany color. The Amazon is a white-water river. That also refers to the color of the water, not to rapids. Amazonian white-water rivers are dense with floating silt, so they look more like weak chocolate milk. They are low in acids. They breed mosquitos and carry more disease. The water requires heavy filtration.

Which is why Dr. Ritta Bernardino stocks a good selection of booze at the Ariau Jungle Tower Lodge. Bernardino, who also owns the Hotel Monaco, is a Manaus lawyer who jumped onto the eco-tourism train in 1986 when he built a wooden tower with a circular parapet that contained a few mosquito-screened rooms thirty-five miles upriver from Manaus. Now the lodge has four towers all connected by wooden walkways placed at midcanopy level and a star-studded guest book testifying to its success.

Bernardino may be one of the few men whose dreams of Amazonian gold have come true. A basic room, a room with two foam-rubber mattresses and cold running water, ran $120 per night when I visited. The water from the river, the same water that supplies the guest rooms, is utterly undrinkable. That means you have to buy bottled water for about two dollars. The room price includes basic buffet meals and guiding services. There are lots of extra charges, too. A phone call on the radio phone will cost you ten dollars per minute. The use of a motorized canoe, thirty dollars per hour. Still, the lodge is in the middle of a rain forest, after all. Operating it is an expensive proposition.

Bernardino though, serves up a slice of cheese at his lodge. He offers a Tarzan suite high in a tree for three hundred dollars per night. He has an Imperial Suite for an unlisted price. He has put a refrigerator, an air conditioner, and a king-sized bed in this suite. There is also an especially attractive black-lacquer bar with gold metallic trim decorated with strategically placed bottles of premium whiskey that seems to have appeared from the top floor of the old Dunes Hotel in Las Vegas. There is even a jewelry store in the bamboo lobby—just in case you fall in love in the jungle and need a quick engagement ring.

Across the wall of the communal dining room, Bernardino has

placed wooden plaques touting the famous people, like Kevin Costner and Lindsay Wagner, who have visited his lodge. The stars are, the wall declares, very important people. It all amounts to an artificial Heart of Darkness with Hollywood cachet and amenities.

But here regular guests can be become a "Defender of the Environment." The lodge hands out certificates that testify all the customers have received "jungle survival training" and have done "reconnaissance." I was proud to receive mine.

Still, I began to question the rigors of the certification process when I saw the Italian tour group climb out of a long dugout canoe. They were, quite simply, the most fashionable people I have ever seen in a jungle. One woman, dressed in strappy gold sandals, slipped on the dock of the Ariau and quickly recovered, brushing the hair back from her sweaty forehead with delicate long fingers. She smiled slightly, a little embarrassed. Another woman's kicky white pants were stained with mud. She walked regally up the wooden stairs anyway, refusing to give an inch to the circumstances. The next day, she and the rest would be off to Río, then São Paulo, places where fashion counts. They had all made a silent pact among themselves to endure this brief stop with Gucci intact.

Alzenir Souza had an intrinsic understanding of this. He knew nobody came to Ariau for a total Amazonian immersion. And as a lodge guide, it was his job to see that the visitors got just enough fantasy without frightening them away. He was very good at this. Later, I wondered why he did not follow that practice with me.

Souza is one generation removed from the bush. His mother was an Amazonian indian. His father was of European descent. He grew up in a small settlement not far from Ariau, living on the river, farming a little, hunting for food. He knew almost nothing about his mother's people. His mother was ashamed of them, he said. They were too primitive, a refrain heard all over the Amazon, where the modern Brazil smacks into the old ways and the rush to convert has induced nearly every Amazonian culture to sprint headlong toward the shining beacons of Pepsi, Michael Jordan, and Marlboro cigarettes.

Souza explained his family history to me as we sat in a canoe fishing for piranha. Only gringos fish for pirhana, of course. They are a trash fish. You can eat them, and locals sometimes will when they have nothing better, but piranha are a nuisance. Tourists like me, our heads full of horrific movie scenes of water boiling with piranha frenzy, with tales of piranha stripping the meat off a man in seconds, love to fish for them. I sure did.

There isn't much skill involved in piranha fishing. The little protein freaks will bite into any matter that resembles flesh. The tackle consists of a short cane pole, a line tied to the pole, a wire leader to prevent the piranha's teeth from severing the line, and a hook. The hook can be baited with any kind of meat. We used chicken. A good piranha fisherman will canoe to still water near shore, preferably with some bushes growing nearby. He will drop the hook in the river, swish the end of the pole through the water to ring the dinner bell, and, when he feels a nibble, set the hook and haul up a fish. You can catch dozens this way. In fact, getting the fish off the hook is the tough part. Some indians used to make scissors from their jaws. I can't think of a better material.

I asked Souza about the tales of men being eaten alive.

"It could happen," he said. "If you get enough of the fish together in one small place and a man swam in the middle of them and didn't swim out, he could be killed. But usually when somebody feels a bite, they swim away and get out of the water."

Usually?

In fact, men are sometimes attacked and suffer bite wounds. More commonly, though, small mammals fall prey to piranha. But a piranha's normal diet is other fish, especially the tails of other fish. Catch a larger species in the basin and you are very likely to see a row of bites off its tail from frequent piranha attacks. The piranha don't often kill these large species. They are content to create tail-fin amputees.

When the daily afternoon storm rose in the west, Souza and I cut short our fishing trip. During the wet season that starts in the late South American summer, the heat rises like a fever throughout the day. Then, as if the sky simply reaches critical mass and cannot absorb another degree or another point of humidity, the fever breaks, and curtains of rain sweep out of the sky.

We reached the lodge just before the storm became intense. I sat in the hammock in the quiet lobby and watched the rain fall. The drops closed off visibility until I felt surrounded by it. And the thoughts came pouring in like the rain.

Traveling had always been a dream of mine when I was a kid sitting in a small Ohio town watching Tarzan movies. I was Jimmy Stewart wanting out of Bedford Falls. But now, sitting on a hammock in the Amazon, looking at the rain, I wondered if I had left something behind as I was looking away, out there. Travel is a drug. It stimulates the senses so fiercely that the new input crowds out all other thoughts, at least for a while. Maybe that's why I had been drawn to rain forests. They are dense, stuffed with strange things and puzzling people, the best drug I had found. And I realized that I always managed to find myself in one soon after a roll of life's dice had sent my token back a few squares. But I had spent five years going to rain forests, and the gnawing urges had not been suppressed. Indeed, from the vantage point of this hammock in the rain in a cheesy lodge in the Amazon, rain forests seemed like a string of odd disappointments. Could the drug wear off? I hoped not. I didn't think so, at least not yet. This was the Amazon, after all, the most powerful drug of all. I needed it to hold out just a little longer.

The rain stopped. I opened my eyes. The sky was nearly dark, and I could barely make out the clouds.

I walked upstairs to the recreation room where I found Guido, a twenty-seven-year-old guide playing Brazilian pool, a game played on a smaller table and using smaller balls than in U.S. pool. One player plays odd numbers, one even. He invited me to play and explained the rules, a set of regulations that achieved remarkable fluidity in Guido's hands.

"What are you doing in the Amazon?" he asked.

"I'm on my way to Tefé," I said.

"Tefé? Nobody goes to Tefé! What do you want in Tefé?"

I thought better of explaining why I was going to Tefé and said that I just wanted to see another part of the Amazon. He shook his head as if to say that some gringos were pretty crazy.

I could tell immediately that Guido was not from Amazonas state. He was tall and handsome in a Placido Domingo way, and carried himself like someone from a city. He did not have a trace of indian blood in his features.

"I'm from Río," he explained. I asked Guido how he managed to find himself in the jungle after living in the city of Cariocas. Usually, I said, the migration goes the other way.

"I just wanted to find some peace," he said. "I thought I might find it in the jungle. Too many criminals in Río." The way he said this made me wonder if there weren't a more complicated, and dangerous, answer. If you wanted to get lost, the Amazon is the place. But given my mood, I understood. Guido was looking for a drug, too.

His command of English won him a spot with Ariau even though he had never seen a jungle before landing in Manaus on a one-way ticket. Guido, it appeared, had followed the tracks of so many others. He wasn't likely to find his fortune, though. He was paid $125 per month. If he could latch onto a guest who was unhappy with a basic room and talk that guest into taking a suite, Guido got ten percent of the suite rate as a bonus. His food and lodging at the tower were provided. He slept in the male dorm. Every two weeks, Guido, like the other guides, went into Manaus to stay at the Hotel Monaco and spend the money he had earned.

Guido said he was just trying to make enough money to buy himself a boat and an outboard. He wanted to take this boat upriver, take it into Venezuela, maybe, or over to Colombia. He wanted to take the boat all the way to the Caribbean. He heard it was nice there. Maybe he'd find some peace.

The jungle wasn't peaceful enough. "It is full of Americans. There are many people in the jungle," he said conspiratorially. "They say they are scientists or tourists." That was logical, I thought, but Guido knew the real truth. "Actually," he continued, "they are spies. They spy for Texaco and Shell Oil and, of course, the CIA."

Of course. After talking to Halim in Malaysia and Teresita in Guatemala and a few odd characters in other jungles, I now knew for certain that the CIA, besides being omnipotent, employed approximately four million Americans.

Guido was explaining just how the First World was plotting to take over the Amazon when Souza walked into the room and said he was going out to hunt for caimans, the crocodilian reptiles that live in great numbers throughout the basin. It was his job to bring a good one back to the lodge to show the guests. He asked if I wanted to come along. Guido said he wanted to come, too.

Finding a caiman is easy. Catching one isn't. We sat in a long dugout canoe. A car battery was placed in front of the boat and a high-intensity spotlight was wired to it. We motored out into the channel that passes in front of the lodge and snaked our way around the vast floating meadows, river grasses that grow in still water during the wet season and provide hiding places for caiman.

Overhead, the sky was alight with stars.

We slowed the motor to a sputter and turned on the light. Souza aimed it at the edges of the grassy islands. Several pairs of shiny golden eyes reflected light back to us. They were caimans. That was the easy part.

Souza stood up in the bow of the canoe and held a staff about four feet long. The end of the staff branched into two arms so that a gap between the arms formed a Y. Souza stretched a piece of rope across the Y. He had created a rigid noose. As we approached the caiman the animal remained remarkably still, seemingly unafraid of the boat or of us. But just when Souza reached over the edge with his noose, the big lizard sank under water.

For the next half hour we hunted caimans under the stars. I didn't much care if we caught one or not, the night was so beautiful. The moon had risen and formed a big disk on the horizon. But Souza is a guide, and he takes his job seriously; and, besides, he grew up hunting caiman for leather and for meat, and he was going to be damned before he'd be skunked.

Finally, when we sidled up to another animal and Souza reached out with his noose, he managed to twitch the thing around the caiman's neck before the animal could slip under the water. The caiman thrashed, but it was small and stood no chance against Souza. Souza lifted it out of the water, then held the caiman under its forelegs to give me a brief anatomy lesson. He pointed out the belly, which yields the best skin for leather and is the meatiest part of the animal, the part his family used to eat. Then Souza let the caiman go.

We had about given up the hunt and had begun slowly motoring toward the lodge when another pair of eyes popped up fifty yards from the boat.

"It's a big one," Souza said under his breath. He wanted it badly, more as a sporting challenge, I think, than for the tourists' education. We skated across the water and reached the edge of a grassy island. We cut the engine, and Souza half-kneeled in the bow. He leaned out farther and farther. Just as he was on the verge of falling, he whapped the noose into the water and half the staff disappeared beneath the surface. I thought he had missed, but the caiman was lassoed and was dragging the noose, and Souza, into the river.

The two creatures of the Amazon battled it out for over a minute. Souza finally wrapped the rope around his forearms, braced his feet on one of the canoe's thwarts, and pulled with every muscle. The caiman, faced with death by choking or giving into

Souza, opted to give in. Souza hauled him aboard, all four feet of him. The canoe was ten feet long.

I thanked Souza for placing the lizard's tail in the bow so his face was about six inches from mine in the middle of the boat. Sixty pounds of agitated crocodile was lying at my feet. This made me a little uncomfortable. The only thing holding it down was Souza's knee in its back. I grabbed the loose end of the rope and handed it to Souza, hoping that would help him tie the caiman a little faster. At least I guessed that's what he had in mind since he wasn't throwing him back. Souza wound the rope around the caiman's snout, closing its mouth, and tied the rope off behind the animal's neck. Souza was satisfied the caiman was secure. I had my doubts, but Souza is, I told myself, a man of the jungle.

The caiman sat like a surly lump of shoe leather. It blinked an eye and quivered just a little.

Suddenly, all hell broke loose. The caiman thrashed its body around the canoe and made a mockery of Souza's knot-tying skills, slipping out of the rope like a man slipping out of his pajamas. All four feet of caiman lunged at me, the only human in its line of sight, and made a green blur as it swung its open mouth at my head.

I dodged its big canines by an inch or so as it slashed by me, aiming for Guido in the stern. Guido, who was now thinking things were a lot more peaceful back in Río, opened his mouth but could not manage a sound. His eyes bulged and he backed up on his hands to the end of the boat. When I finally realized I was not going to be caiman food, I grabbed the animal's tail and yanked backward. Caimans, I discovered, have very strong tails. Guido was swearing in Portuguese and debating the risks of swimming with the piranha or staying in a boat with a loose caiman when Souza jumped on the lizard like a heroic soldier throwing himself on a grenade. Souza, a slightly built half-indian, weighed maybe 140 pounds. It was barely enough. I held the lizard's tail, at least as much out of fear as for any effect it might have, while Souza kneeled on its back and swung the rope around its snout. I looked at Souza.

"We've tried this," I said, a little out of breath.

He made double knots and tied the rope so tightly I began to fear for the caiman. Guido, meanwhile, was rethinking his desire to boat to Venezuala.

When we reached the lodge, two guests appeared, took a quick picture, and returned to the books they were reading in the hammock. Didn't they appreciate the epic duel? I wanted to grab them by the scruff of the neck and ask them exactly how easy they thought it was to haul in a full-grown caiman.

The other guides, though, were ecstatic. Each young man took turns holding the caiman and flexing biceps and standing on the caiman's back with arms raised in the air. Guido even became emboldened. He lifted the animal's tail while a friend snapped a picture. Maybe he would send that back to Río, he said. Show his friends what it was like in the jungle. The caiman just sat, resting on the small dock until the teenage paparazzi finished. Then it trotted off into the river.

I left the lodge early in the morning. The boat docked back in Manaus in the heat of the mid-morning rush. It was raining, a little earlier than usual, and it appeared as though it might rain all day. I called Varig, an airline I had come to love. It flew on time and its flight attendants smiled. To me, that was all anybody could ask. But now, on the phone from the docks, I heard that the line had let me down. It had cancelled my flight to Tefé. Today was a holiday, it said, so the flight was suspended.

This was a crock. It was, in fact, a holiday. Brazilians were commemorating a military battle from the last century, one of a long series that were fought over borderlines. Brazil had won this one.

But I was holding a ticket, one I had confirmed two days before, and the ticket said today. I could see airplanes taking off from Manaus airport, I screamed into the phone.

"But why would you want to go to Tefé?" said the voice at the other end. "Nobody goes to Tefé."

Now it was becoming clear. This was why Varig had cancelled the flight. Nobody does go to Tefé. At least not on my flight. I was, it seemed, the only booked passenger, so the airline had cancelled the stop and called it a holiday.

I was angry because I had made plans to be in Tefé on this day to hop a boat that would take me upriver into the bush. I had already had some doubts about this plan. Confirmation seemed to be nebulous, and I knew there was some poor communication. And now I was going to be at least a day late.

And I was stranded in Manaus, a city I had grown to loathe, and facing a walk up to the showplace that is the Hotel Monaco. Then I remembered that Varig owned the Hotel Tropical.

"Look," I said, "put me up in the Tropical and get me a flight out tomorrow." Varig flies only twice per week to Tefé but another line, TABA, flies daily in tiny propeller commuters. The voice agreed, and I was on my way to the Tropical, where I expected to find Gary and Russell ensconced with two tearful chamber maids, a bottle of Scotch, and a boom box playing bossa nova.

Instead I found a lobby stuffed with tourists, a row of stores selling fake indian artifacts and *guaraná* powder (thought to be a stimulant), a giant swimming pool, a small zoo with caged Amazonian animals, and, after a very long hike, my room. The front desk had informed me that making the early TABA flight would mean I would have to meet a bus at 4:30 A.M. in front of the hotel, so I thought I'd take a walk around the grounds, have some dinner, and go to sleep. I walked outside to watch the sun set over the Negro. I returned to my room and tried to call my contacts in Tefé. I reached them. They had never heard of me. They weren't prepared for me. Maybe I should not come. I hung up.

I started feeling a little like the Martin Sheen character in *Apoc-*

olypse Now, waiting here to go into the jungle to find . . . what? Colonel Kurtz? Exotic women? A bad case of ameobic dysentery?

Just when I was feeling importantly overwrought, I turned on the television. A music video by a Brazilian rap/samba group (trust me) called Fausto Fawcett blared out of my set. The song was "Basico Instinto," or Basic Instinct. It featured half a dozen video bimbos in revealing leather shorts and G-strings who spent most of their screen time trying to touch their toes. I was convinced that the group financed the recording of this song solely for the chance to audition the women. I changed channels and was immediately confronted with mating elephants. It was a documentary about love. The bull elephant was about to demonstrate his affection for the cow using his massive prehensile penis. Click. Alvin and the Chipmunks were starring in "Gone Fishin'." Click. Elton John and a transvestite, RuPaul, were singing a duet called "Don't Go Breakin' My Heart." Click. Back to the documentary. The Wadaabe people of Sierra Leone had gone a-courting. The men, it seems, dress up in finery and wear makeup to compete for the love of the women. "Love," the narrator said, "is the most important communication of our lives." Click. The rock group Alice in Chains was singing its hit "Down in a Hole."

I became hysterical with laughter. I seemed to be at the center of some absurd vortex. I figured I would just go with it.

From the time I was little, I thought flying in an airplane was a kind of miracle, and since I had begun travelling to remote areas, the thought of flying to virtually unheard of villages had always floored me. As a result, I am normally very easy-going when it comes to snafus. Can't fly today? So what. It's wild that you ever fly there at all.

But when I arrived at the Manaus airport in the early-morning darkness and was told by the Varig counter agent whom I had asked for my TABA voucher that Varig couldn't possibly have made such an arrangement, he feared for his life. There was no way I was leaving that counter without that voucher. He was actually scared. He called a supervisor. "I will fly to Tefé," I said. "You WILL get me on that flight." My knuckles were locked in a white grip around the edge of the counter, and I think they suspected I was ready to lunge. I was. They made a couple of frantic phone calls and quickly wrote up a voucher.

They neglected to tell me, however, that TABA was not located at the airport in which I was now standing. The Varig desk agent waited to relay this shocking news until I returned, breathless and perspiring, and begged him to tell me where to find the airline. "Oh," he said with a smile, "TABA is not in this airport. They are in the old airport." The old airport was located half a mile away, beyond the cargo terminal. "You will not make their flight," he said still smiling, "unless you run very fast."

This is why the U.S. needs better gun control. Today, people are alive in Brazil because I did not have a weapon.

The old airport is what one might expect in Manaus. It was small and offered one gate. I made it to this gate just as the ticket agent and only TABA employee in sight was collecting boarding passes from my eight fellow passengers. Four of us, myself included, were going to Tefé. Whadda ya know, I thought, some people DO go to Tefé. But they don't go smiling. There was an Amazonas state bureaucrat who was clearly very unhappy to be boarding this plane, a very clean-cut Brazilian man in polyester trousers and a striped business shirt who looked suspiciously like a missionary, and a Brazilian medical worker who carried a Coleman Playmate cooler wrapped in strapping tape and labeled CAUTION: VACCINE in Portuguese, Spanish, and English. I took this group as a bad sign about Tefé.

The plane was an old Brazilian-made twin-engine puddle-jumper. I sat just behind the cockpit across the aisle from the bureaucrat. There was a seat in front of him, filled by a TABA employee who read a joke book. We taxied away from the tarmac

of being lost in its jungles and felt a twinge of excitement at the thought. Now, cruising above the Amazon, I realized for the first time since I had been in Brazil that my mind would not be able to reach around the Amazon and even begin to take it in. Intellectually I knew how much life there was down there. Viscerally, it seemed like a lonely, desolate, scary place.

When we began to descend, I remembered that this trip could turn out to be a disaster. I had no idea if anybody in Tefé even knew or cared that I would be arriving. My plan was to just show up and see what happened.

But there, just beyond the doorway to the tiny concrete block terminal that sat at the end of the airstrip, was a thin, nervous man with scraggly sideburns, glasses and a brown leather fedora. He was clutching a small plastic toiletries bag labeled ENGLISH LAVENDER. As the only gringo, I was not hard to spot.

"Mr. Brian!" the man called out.

By now I was used to my first name being switched to become my last, especially in Brazil, where Alexander is a common first name. I walked through the door and reached out to shake hands.

"I am La-fay-etchay," he said. It would take two days before I realized his name was Layfayette, Layfayette MacCullough, a spelling and pronunciation some Scottish ancestor would hardly recognize.

Finally, I thought, something was going my way. Lafayette, I knew, was the Tefé manager of Projecto Mamirauá (ma-MEER-uhwow), the environmental project I had come to see. His was the voice on the crackly phone connection that had disclaimed any knowledge of me the night before. I introduced myself and understood immediately that Lafayette was here but still had no idea who I was or why I was here and didn't want the complication of finding out. His life was complicated enough.

After I grabbed my duffel from the wooden counter that served as the luggage carousel, Lafayette led me to a taxi. Actually he led me to THE taxi. No roads lead to Tefé and the only way to get a was going and couldn't avoid potholes and ruts. This was transportation by Braille. The only way to tell if you were on the road at all was by looking through the floor, which was pretty easy to do.

All this only added to the bureaucrat's distress. He was trying to remain officious-looking in his brown suit, but he obviously hated being in Tefé, this foreign country within a country. Carlos though, was very happy. And why not? He owned the taxi. It was capable of forward motion. In Tefé, that was something. Life was good.

Carlos knew Lafayette and so knew exactly where to go: the "Project House." Projecto Mamirauá was based in a former private home, the nicest home available, a white stucco, vaguely Spanish-style, two-story building two blocks off Tefé's main street. Carlos dropped us off in front of a high stucco wall interrupted by an arched gateway, which was shut off by large flat iron doors. An iron sign outside designated the house "Sociedad Civil Mamirauá." Lafayette pulled out some keys and unlocked a smaller door carved out of the big iron gates.

My eyes darted immediately to the swimming pool. That was a pretty nice amenity, I thought to myself, until I walked a step or two and saw beyond the pool's rim. About three feet of inky water sat pouting in the deep end, fermenting a collection of mosses and leaves. A minor cloud of mosquitoes buzzed over the water. I asked Lafayette about the pool. He shrugged.

"We got this house because it had a pool. Marcio likes to swim," he explained, referring to Dr. Marcio Ayres, the man behind Projecto Mamirauá.

"But it doesn't work?"

"No, it has never worked. No parts. Maybe parts will come in months."

A gleaming Land Rover sat next to the pool. It was donated by the British, who were major contributors to the project. There was not a nick out of the paint, and the tires were just off the

car into town is by riverboat, so cars were something of an
This oddity was owned by a fellow named Carlos, a big
man whose face was permanently inscribed with a wide
revealed every spot in his mouth where teeth should b
Carlos' black hair was shiny with perspiration, his old sh
shirt was wet with it, and his brown double-knit pants sp
it. He wore brown loafers that had somehow walked al
Tefé from wherever they were made. He wore no sock

Since there was only one taxi in Tefé, everybody
bureaucrat climbed in the front and Lafayette and I sq
back. This was a complicated process because the pa
did not open from the outside. Carlos had to kick
the taxi to fling it open. Carlos climbed in first
avoiding an illegal act with the stick shift, slammed
the passenger door and invited us in like the d
Piérre Hotel. Lafayette contorted himself into an ir
to ooze past the front seat. I bent double and plur
to Lafayette. Finally, the bureaucrat sat in front, gr
briefcase on his lap and no doubt wondering
offended back in Manaus to deserve this assig
were all in position, Carlos stretched his arm o
window like a teenager showing off his new
cruising toward town.

Carlos' taxi was a miracle of perseverance. F
it would have been shot in a mercy killing. Th
Toyota. The actual make was hard to determi
the only sign that a brand name had ever been
or side body panel. No gauges worked. T
worked. Several, like the speedometer, had r
trious farmer could have brought in a crop f
The car may have had shock absorbers at on
not now, which was probably just as well
shock absorber on Tefé's roads would hav
utes. The windshield was so filthy that Car

factory line. I looked in the passenger-side window. The drive shaft sat in the front seat.

"What happened?" I asked, pointing inside the truck.

"It's broken."

"Yes, but how long?"

"About six months."

"Six months?"

"Yes. There seems to be a problem with parts. They have to come from England."

"When do you think more parts will come?"

"Maybe six months."

Lafayette and I walked up the staircase that hung on the outside of the house to the second story. We entered the tiny, linoleumed foyer with its beat-up sofa and TV and went into the kitchen. There was a refrigerator, a gas stove, a sink, and scores of plastic bottles of water. The municipal supply, Lafayette said, was undrinkable unless you dripped it through a clay filter pot. Even then, it was dicey if you were not used to it. Lafayette offered me some coffee, which I gratefully accepted. Lafayette poured some that had been sitting on the stove into a big carafe and set it on the table with some bread. I was beginning to feel better—comfortable, almost. Lafayette sat down across the table from me.

"What do you want here?" he asked.

Oh, right. There was that little problem. I began to explain who I was and why I was here, but Lafayette only looked confused. He spoke no English so we had been communicating in a kind of Spanguese. I would speak Spanish very slowly, which was the only way I could speak Spanish, and he would speak Portuguese very slowly, and since the two languages are so similar, I would understand about every other word. So far it had worked, but all we had discussed was broken parts. Now our system broke down. I started over. I told him who I was. I told him why I was here. I told him I was supposed to go upriver on one of the project's boats. I could see he was beginning to understand, but he was not liking any of it. Finally, I pulled out an old fax from Ayres which repeated everything I had just told him. This was a good thing except Lafayette could not read English.

He got up from the table carrying the fax and disappeared.

Another wave of depression slammed into my head. This was starting to trouble me. I was rarely depressed and never when traveling, especially to rain forests, but I could not seem to shake off the enveloping funk. I got up out of my seat, holding my cup of Brazilian coffee, and stood at the back kitchen window looking out into the hugely overgrown backyard and the hovels on either side of the house. There, on the mud and brick walls separating the houses, sat a long row of tremendous black vultures all hunched with their bald heads peering back at me. That cheered me right up.

Lafayette returned to the kitchen with Dr. Miriam Marmontel in tow. She sat down at the table. I asked her in Spansh if she spoke English. She smiled.

"Well, I speak pretty good American," she said.

And she did, too, without the slightest hint of an accent.

"You're from the States?" I asked.

"No, I'm Brazilian, but I lived there."

Miriam had been a high-school exchange student in New England and later returned to study in a university in Florida. In fact, she had been in Tefé only a few months since she had left her apartment in Key Biscayne, which, I reckoned, must have created a powerful cultural whiplash. In addition to speaking excellent American, Miriam had a Yankee sense of directness.

"Look," she said. "We do not know who you are. Nobody here was expecting you."

"I kind of figured that one out," I replied, "but these plans have been set for months. Marcio and I have exchanged a lot of faxes. He knew when I was coming."

Which, of course, did nobody in Tefé the slightest good. Ayres lived in Belém, as in the other end of Brazil. He had somehow neglected to tell anybody in Tefé about me.

"That's really not too unusual," Miriam said with a sigh. "What do you want us to do?"

I told her about my intentions to go into the Mamirauá reserve, live there in the floating house, watch researchers, meet locals, and generally be a big nuisance to scientists who hate people looking over their shoulders. Miriam frowned. She conferred with Lafayette. She frowned again and looked at the fax. She looked at me and yammered in Portuguese again with Lafayette. Finally she turned to me.

"The problem is that there is nobody available to take you into the reserve, and the local people are very suspicious of outsiders. Also, we are short of supplies and boats. But if you can wait until tomorrow, I will go with you."

I got the distinct feeling Miriam was not at all happy about going into the reserve with me. She had work to do in Tefé, and making the trip upriver was not part of her plans. She seemed like a very serious woman, too serious, even, and I figured a little fawning might go a long way. I told her how appreciative I was, that I knew how inconvenient it must be for her, and that I did not mean to steal time away from her research. I meant it, too. In fact, I considered picking up my bag and heading back to Manaus. Either the world was out of sorts or I was. Either way, retreat seemed like a good idea.

But Miriam began to probe how much I knew about rain forests and about várzea in particular. She seemed surprised, and pleased, I knew anything at all. She actually smiled, briefly, revealing a perfect set of white teeth that shone against her deeply tanned brown skin and long black hair. There was a good video, she said, of the várzea. Maybe I would like to watch it while she made some plans for tomorrow?

She slipped the video into the VCR, and I sat in the foyer watching.

About three percent of the Amazon consists of *várzea*, lowland riverine forests that flood yearly, turning the trees into stalkless broccoli tops surrounded by water. While the three-percent figure may not seem like much, it roughly equals about 150,000 square kilometers, an area the size of the state of Georgia. And, according to biologists, its importance to the overall Amazonian ecosystem is far out of proportion to its size. Because its watery environment is unique compared to upland, or terra firma, forests, scientists speculate that plant and animal species have had to adapt. The *arauana*, for example, is a fish that lives in *várzea*. When it spots, say, a beetle sitting on a tree branch, the *arauana* can leap completely out of the water and snatch the beetle off the tree, which is why locals call it the "monkey fish." Sometimes, say scientists, new species result and are carried out of the *várzea*, winding up as part of a terra firma system.

Some argue that the *várzea* is also a genetic refuge. The *boto*, one of two freshwater dolphin species in the region, is a primitive member of the dolphin family. It lives primarily in flooded forests during the seven months of inundation and is able to forage among the submerged roots and underwater bushes thanks to its superior echolocation abilities and a flexible neck no other dolphins have. These forests are also a haven for the only totally freshwater manatees in the world. The indian name for these aquatic mammals is *mamirauá*.

One scientist has suggested that only fifteen percent of the *várzea* on the lower two thousand kilometers of the Amazon remains. One problem is soil. The soil in the *várzea* is much richer than soil in upland forests, making it prized for grazing land during the dry months when the water recedes. In all, about six percent of Amazonian forest has been cleared, an area of over 325,000 square kilometers. If that level of destruction is transferred to *várzea* regions so cattle can munch better grass, as some have suggested doing, it would take very little time to wipe out the entire *várzea* system.

That may happen anyway. Because you can't build a road into the *várzea,* and since, during the months of inundation, you have to cut timber from a canoe and float the logs out from under the canopy, loggers discovered these areas late in the search for tropical hardwoods. But commercial timber interests have caught on and already removed many of the largest *samaumeira, assacu,* and kapok trees.

Fishing fleets present another threat. The waters around Manaus have been overfished, so fishing boats are venturing farther upriver with huge seine nets that can wipe out a lake in days.

Both of these forces were acting on a huge chunk of *várzea* at the junction of the Japurá and Solimões rivers in western Amazonas state. That was also an area where Ayres, a Brazilian biologist, a specialist in primates, was conducting a survey and discovering that the range of the uakari (waa-CAR-ee), a red-faced monkey with long white fur (also called the English monkey because its red face reminded locals of Englishmen after a day in the equatorial sun), exactly matched the area of *várzea* between the two rivers on the north and south and the Auati-Paraná river channel on the west. Ayres wanted to preserve it.

He was lucky. First, he was politically connected. Second, the photogenic uakari gave him a perfect poster child to campaign for a *várzea* reserve. Brazil designated the uakari's range—2,000 square kilometers, about 780 square miles—as an ecological station in 1990 and named it Mamirauá. Now, about eighty international researchers, only ten of whom lived full-time in Tefé, were trying to figure out what was in Mamirauá and how to save it.

Neither of which was going to be easy. The *várzea* was largely a mystery. Few had made any serious studies of it. Even the maximum and minimum water levels remained a puzzle. Nobody, except perhaps the local people living there, called Caboclos, knew what was there—how many previously undescribed species of fish, mammals, plants, or insects might be floundering in the watery forests. There were lots of monkeys, including red howlers, capuchins, and, of course, the uakari. The three-toed sloth lived in the *várzea,* rarely coming down from the tree tops. Jaguar lived there and so did capybaras, the world's largest rodent.

So did the Caboclos. They were a mélange of indian, African and European blood and had lived in the *várzea* for hundreds of years. They were cutting and fishing and hunting, too. Ayres, against some strong criticism, opted to leave the Caboclos in their stilted shacks, reasoning that they could be transformed into on-site park rangers, that they could be convinced that their very lives depended upon a healthy ecosystem. Ayres was hoping long-term self-interest would outweigh destructive habits. It was a big gamble. Mamirauá was the only preserve in Brazil where locals were allowed to stay in place. But Ayres knew that it was one thing to declare a preserve but another to enforce that declaration in a country where there was one park ranger for every 366,000 square kilometers of protected area. Ayres figured every Caboclo could be a de facto ranger. There were, of course, real park rangers. Two of them. They lived in Tefé. They had a boat to get into the reserve. The boat had not worked in two years.

The mayor of Tefé liked that. He owned the local sawmill.

There was a bedroom off to the side of the foyer that contained four bunks. I was stowing my gear under one of them when a young man who looked remarkably like Che Guevera dashed into the room, swore in Portuguese, and dashed back out again. He was perspiring, of course, since by 10 A.M. the temperature was at least ninety degrees and everyone walked around perspiring at all times, but he was also very agitated. He ran back downstairs and into a door on the first floor, then ran back up again. He stared at me wide-eyed, and I wondered if he might be a crazed scientist. Which is exactly what he was.

"Where is Lafayette?" he asked in Portuguese.

"I don't know," I answered in English. This stopped him for a moment as he realized for the first time that we had never met.

"Hello," he said in careful broken English. "I am Pedro dos Santos. I am very sorry. I am in a large hurry."

With that he sprinted back into the bedroom, snatched a backpack from the top of the closet, and ran down the stairs and out into the street.

Lafayette peeked out of the downstairs doorway. He looked around the courtyard as if looking for hidden assassins. Once he saw the coast was clear, he climbed the steps, patted me on the shoulder, sighed, and walked into the house.

Tefé sat on a big lake, Lago Tefé, at the mouth of the Tefé River, a tributary of the Solimões. Tefé's location near the confluence of the Japurá and Solimões made it a convenient spot for a late-1800s western Amazonia entrepot. The town itself was built up on a bank of the lake and sloped upward from the shore. The project house was situated at the top of the rise, the new suburbs, while most of the town was down by the water.

It was hard to tell which streets were dust and which were paved since the three or four paved streets were covered with a fine silt. The houses were mostly one-story tumbledowns made of stucco. Many had neither doors nor glass in the window frames. Sewage was a problem. Gutters carrying raw sewage ran between the edge of the streets and what passed for a sidewalk. In places, square concrete slabs had been laid over the gutters to make tiny bridges across the fetid streams so a pedestrian could walk from sidewalk to street without having to jump over the deep trenches. An al fresco nightclub half a block from the project house did a pretty good business. A dozen or so empty Antarctica beer bottles were scattered around the stools and tables. There was another nightclub just a few doors away.

Tefé was not the kind of town that could normally support two nightclubs, not even these tiny bistros where the entertainment came from boom boxes placed in front of a microphone. But Tefé had recently been designated as a major army post. There were dozens of troops strolling around in uniform. Some were not in uniform but were given away by their military-style haircuts. These soldiers, who usually had a local girl on one arm, came from The South and spent their desultory days playing soccer and drilling and drinking beer. But they were in Tefé to defend the jungle against the First World invasion Brazil feared might pour down out of a northern hemisphere desperate for miracle drugs and forest preservation.

"They say they are here to stop the cocaine trade," Miriam said, "but they are really here to prevent the internationalization of the rain forest."

Sometimes the soldiers fought intense mock jungle battles. Brazil took the idea of an ecological war seriously.

Pedro raced back into the house, swearing and sweating once again.

"No crew! There is no crew! La-fay-etchay! Where is my crew?"

Lafayette bent his shoulders, stared at the floor, and scratched the back of his neck.

"You have no crew?"

"I have some crew. I am missing people."

"Can you go without them?"

"No!"

"Then you will have to wait. Maybe they were confused about when you wanted to go?"

Pedro turned to me and, in English, explained that he was to have been on his way upriver early this morning. The boat was not ready. Now that the boat was ready, the crew was not there.

"It is always like this. This is crazy! How can we work?"

Pedro ran back out again. Lafayette smiled at me and slapped on his brown leather fedora and photosensitive glasses, picked up his now-bulging English Lavender bag and motioned for me to follow.

Carlos was waiting outside with his smile and his shoes and his miracle car. We climbed in and lurched our way toward the center of town. Lafayette ordered Carlos to stop in front of a small store and then leaped out of the car, scurried into the store and returned a moment later with a cardboard box full of water bottles. Another block down the street and we stopped again and Lafayette ran into another store and came back with a load of bananas and some vegetables. He piled all these items in the back seat, where I was sitting. At the next stop he retrieved a huge bag of rice. He was a whirlwind. At no time did money ever leave Lafayette's hands and when I looked at the plastic English Lavender bag, I discovered why. The bag was Lafayette's lifeline, a filing system stuffed with pieces of paper—receipts, notes, and small chits Lafayette passed around town as IOUs.

Once Lafayette had twirled through town, Carlos dropped us off at one of Tefé's docks on the lake and we tiptoed across a wooden board that connected the bank to the dock. We stood at the end of the dock waiting for, I presumed, a boat.

The dock was an object lesson in public health. A wilting stench floated over the end of the wooden platform, coming from a three-sided enclosure made of plywood. Inside the enclosure, a hole had been cut in the dock, revealing the lake a few inches below. The hole was stained with gobs of shit. This was Tefé's public toilet. Four young boys swam about three feet off the end of the dock.

I pointed to the outhouse and Lafayette nodded, crinkling his nose. I waved my hand at the boys swimming and Lafayette raised his hands and shrugged his shoulders, a gesture that said "That's life in Tefé."

"We have tried to tell them about the cholera," he said, referring to the epidemic that had spread throughout Amazonia two years before and had become an endemic part of existence there.

By the time the aluminum outboard boat pulled up alongside the dock, the wind had kicked up, making for a bumpy ride.

Lafayette looked as comfortable as a socialite at a tractor pull. He kept one hand on his hat and another on his seat until we landed at a small, floating island of planks and two-by-fours that served as the project's carpentry shed and gas dock. Two outboard engines lay in pieces on the boards. Two men were pounding nails into what looked like specimen tables for a lab. There was much gesticulating and watch-glancing, and Lafayette was frustrated over something. In the middle of his conversation, the sky's fever broke and it began to rain, which only made the workmen happy but sent Lafayette scurrying for cover in the minuscule tool shed where a PetroBras calendar showed off girls the Brazilian national oil company felt looked especially good without bikini tops.

Lafayette was exasperated. Lafayette, in fact, was always exasperated. It seemed obvious that he was close to becoming a nervous wreck. Life in a jungle frontier town clearly did not agree with him. Perhaps he did not expect Tefé when Ayres asked him to take over the local management of the project. Perhaps he did not realize the difficulties of organizing and planning the logistics, massaging the scientific egos. He had, the story went, been managing an apartment house in Belém. Belém is a modern city. It has real public toilets and a big airport. But Lafayette had moved to Tefé anyway, maybe for the adventure of it. Maybe to escape his wife.

There were advantages. In Tefé, Lafayette was one of the most important residents in town. He was armed with $4.3 million, which will buy you a lot of importance in a place like Tefé. Local girls seemed pretty impressed. Lafayette fell in love frequently, a habit that annoyed the staff, especially the time when Lafayette decided to play Flo Ziegfeld.

Lafayette, it seemed, had fallen for a girl who wanted to enter Tefé's Brazil nut festival beauty pageant but could not pay the fee. Lafayette thought the project should sponsor the girl, strictly for public relations, of course, and he, naturally, should be her coach. Lafayette spent weeks working very closely with his protégée, grooming her for stardom on the Tefé stage. When the big day arrived, Lafayette gave his candidate high-heeled shoes to better seduce the judges, but the poor girl, who had never worn high-heeled shoes, fell on her rear end to howls of laughter. She never spoke to Lafayette again. Lafayette was crushed.

When the rain let up, we returned to shore and walked to the Restaurante Amazonia, the best place in Tefé. We ordered a couple of cold Antarcticas and a plate of fried *tambaqui*, a delicious fruit-eating fish. The fish and rice and beans and beer seemed to wipe away the cloud that had hung over me since I'd left Fortaleza. Finally, for the first time since I had arrived, I was glad to be in the Amazon.

Pedro ran into the restaurant and sat next to Lafayette. His boat did not have fuel. But he was getting fuel. Maybe they could leave soon. Pedro left. Lafayette smiled. Pedro, he said, had not adjusted to the Amazon.

"He is Portuguese. Very European. He is always worried. He thinks he will get malaria. He is always taking the quinine." Lafayette imitated Pedro gulping quinine. Europeans always worried about disease, he said.

The western Amazon was a place where worrying about disease was worry that was wasted. You would get sick, or you would not. Here, people believed in fate, even courted disaster. The passengers on the *Captain Nuñes X* did. As I ate, I looked out the restaurant's window at the largest of the two municipal docks where the *Nuñes X* was pulling in, completing its two-night trip from Manaus. Like all the Amazonian riverboats, it was a garishly painted wooden vessel. At least two hundred people were on its decks. Hammocks had been tied between posts, boxes were stacked everywhere, and the plastic garbage bags and netted sacks people used for luggage were strewn from stem to stern. The boat's bottom deck was barely inches above the water line. One errant wave would have swamped it. It was a sight that would make one wonder about the fate of the previous nine *Captain Nuñes*es.

This part of Tefé, the port and the old center, was still the heart of the city. The town market sprawled just down the sloping, cracked street from the docks. This was the permanent market. Once or twice per week, another market took place in the early morning hours on the lakefront where people who had collected fruits and manioc and some odds and ends gathered to sell. But the main Tefé market was the place to buy meat, vegetables, hammocks. Outdoor markets in hot, humid places always reek, but the Tefé market was a nuclear bomb of aroma. Fish are the biggest part of people's diet in this part of Amazonia; and the *tambaqui*, the giant pirarucu, and several species of catfish lay on tables and hung from hooks silently rotting in the heat. The rough-cut joints of meat and seared pigs heads just added complexity to the bouquet. Flies were thick. People were thin.

As the sun began sliding past its peak directly overhead, tremendous flocks of vultures whirled into the superheated sky, forming black tornados that circled endlessly over the town. Vultures sat at the edges of wooden garbage cans and plucked trophies out of the rubbish. In the town cemetery vultures sat on crosses and tombstones and a remarkable eight-foot-tall pair of pink praying hands.

Things became ghostly at night, the old section a decaying paean to dreams. The buildings, some dating from the 1800s, had not lived up to the expectations of their builders. The old customs house, a long-abandoned dark sandstone structure by the lakeshore, had the same shiny green patina that covered the buildings in Manaus. So did the remains of the nearby monastery that was supposed to have turned indians into priests.

An empty piece of ground near the customs house was covered in rusting amusement rides. A tiny carousel held little metal bucket seats by chains from the center of the machine. A few brown child-size horses sat on the ground. When the wind came up, it whistled through the miniature rides. A dank urine smell flowed between the rides and the bar next door where a few soldiers and locals drank beer.

Two small, mangy dogs stood fornicating in front of the customs house, mocking the grand designs of empire builders, the civilizers of the Amazon. And, I thought, they were mocking me, my pretensions in going to jungles looking for adventure and definition. The male turned his head and stared at me between thrusts. "Fuck you. Go home."

At 8:30 the next morning I stood with Lafayette at the boat dock loading supplies into a thirty-foot-long riverboat. Miriam was there in shorts, a muscle T-shirt, a red bandana, and a huge diver's knife strapped to her leg. She was an imposing figure of jungle womanhood. But she was not happy. We were supposed to have left by 7:30.

I apologized again, though Lafayette was the target of her anger.

"Don't worry," she said. "I have things I need to do in the forest, and it turned out we need the boat at the site so it's not an inconvenience. It would have had to go anyway. . . . La-fay-etchay!"

Lafayette had been climbing back up the bank toward town, but stopped dead.

"La-fay-etchay!"

He returned to the dock like a scolded boy. Miriam indicated our supplies, especially the five-gallon drums of water. Getting filtered water was difficult and became something of an obsession for researchers going into the várzea. There were no supplies of water there at all, ironically enough, since the rivers carried all sorts of disease vectors and parasites from elsewhere in the basin. Miriam argued that we did not have enough because we would be joining two fish researchers at the floating house who would need their own water.

Lafayette stared down at the dock, scratched the back of his neck, and assured her that we had plenty of water. The British had their own.

Miriam insisted we did not.

They bickered like two old married people.

Lafayette won the debate and we pushed off, only to stop a few yards away at a floating gas dock. This did nothing good for Miriam's mood. She interrogated the boat's pilot, one of two Caboclo crewmen on board, who informed Miriam that the boat was virtually empty.

"La-fay-etchay!"

The Caboclos laughed.

We pulled away from the gas dock, where we had filled up on deisel and began the journey to Mamirauá. I was skeptical the boat would make it. The vessel was astonishingly underpowered with an old four-cylinder Yamaha engine coughing *ka-chunk, ka-chunk, ka-chunk* and making agonizingly slow progress against the current. The engine was held together with rubber hoses and bent pieces of metal fashioned, no doubt, by the men working on the project's island of planks in the lake. Like Carlos' taxi, the three gauges in front of the pilot upstairs did not come close to working. Very little of the engine's exhaust actually left the boat. It filled the lower deck with acrid blue smoke.

But Miriam and I sat outside on the top deck in front of the pilothouse and felt the intense sun on our skin. The sky was a sapphire blue, and ten minutes after leaving the gas dock, we were out of Lago Tefé and onto the jungle-lined Solimões. It was a stunningly beautiful day.

Miriam parted her tough curtain ever so slightly and warmed up a little. She told me about what I was seeing and explained the Caboclos.

The Caboclos, she said, had an average income of about fifty dollars per month per family. A typical family had about ten children. Many died before adulthood. When a young man matured, he would find a mate and build a shack near his father's. This had gone on for a couple hundred years. The result was that each village of a dozen or so households was really an extended family group. It also meant you were pretty likely to marry a cousin. If you happened to meet a woman from another village, she had to move to yours and undergo a few years of suspicion before she was truly accepted.

Naturally, some young men had the urge for sex before they caught the urge for marriage. Sometimes a girl would turn up pregnant. Fortunately, there was a legend that *tucuxi*, the other species of river dolphins, transformed themselves into handsome Don Juans at night and came ashore to seduce girls. When a girl turned up pregnant without benefit of a husband, the *tucuxi* took the blame and everybody's virtue was preserved.

Most of the villages in the project area had trouble accepting Mamirauá. They had heard rumors, linked to the British financing, that the scheme was a plot by the British to steal all the fish from their rivers and lakes and ship them to Europe. Most did not know exactly where Europe was, but they knew white men came from there and that was good enough. And they already feared the fishermen from Manaus, the ones who carried rifles and shot at the Caboclos when the locals tried to stop them from seine netting. So outsiders were not welcome at first.

Over time, though, much of the project's work had paid off. Projecto Mamirauá decided not to wait for benefits to begin for Caboclos. The project made a conscious effort to hire villagers whenever possible as cooks, boat pilots, laborers, guides. The ones hired suddenly made more money and ate better than they ever had in their lives. Some had gotten fat, in fact, something one never saw in a Caboclo.

The only village in the project area that was still reticent was also the only village that had been reached by evangelical missionaries.

"They just wave their Bibles around all the time," Miriam said. "They are convinced we are bad people."

But the most stubborn obstacle was the same cast of characters that bedeviled rain forests everywhere. The Amazonas state governor did not support the project; he was in the pocket of commercial interests in Manaus where all the voters were. The federal environment ministry had hired the two rangers, but they were locals, related to families living in Mamirauá. The project had to pay them to go into the preserve when conflicts arose between loggers and Caboclos and take them on a project boat since their own did not work; and even when they did make it into the preserve, they returned to Tefé carting delicacies like eggs from endangered turtles. Worse, they brought liquor into the preserve. Caboclos liked liquor. They liked it far too much, in fact. As a result, booze was supposed to be totally banned.

We *ka-chunked* into the preserve about three hours after leaving Lago Tefé. We plowed through the wide spot in the forest formed by the junction of the Japurá and Solimões, a watery intersection several miles across. Then we headed straight into the forest, up the narrow, rain-swollen Mamirauá River, a watery road through the middle of the preserve. The jungle on either side was flooded, the bottom two-thirds of large trees submerged in the waters. Boca do Mamirauá, or Mouth of the Mamirauá, passed by on our right. Miriam said the village was a keystone for the project since residents could see up and down the rivers and out into the junction. They could warn of approaching fishing boats or strangers entering the preserve. The project had built a small antenna for a short wave radio and trained a man to use it to call Tefé.

Half an hour later we pulled up to the floating house, a near-copy of a large Tennessee hillbilly shack, that floated on a set of giant logs and was tied with rope to the nearest large tree. Will and Pete sat on the front porch, lacking only a jug of moonshine, overalls, and corncob pipes.

But they were shirtless, their very British skin presenting an astonishing reflected brilliance. Will, the younger of the two men, was about twenty-four years old, thin, tall, with curly brown hair. He could have been Stan Laurel's grandson. Pete was forty, blond, pudgy, and may have been the inspiration for the uakari's nickname.

Both of them carried that astonishing British resilience, that sense of propriety that lingers even in the wilderness thousands of miles away from tea at Claridge's Hotel, that stubborness that insists the world around them adapt to their Britishness rather than adapting themselves to the world. Robert Scott no doubt thought the weather a bit chilly as he turned into a frozen Popsicle on his way back from the South Pole. Pete and Will simply sat on the porch and sweated as if sitting on a Hyde Park bench on a cool day.

I admired them instantly.

"Did you bring the water, Miriam?" asked Pete before we were even tied up.

"I brought some," she answered with a question in her voice.

"Lafayette didn't tell you we did not bring water with us?"

This sent Miriam into a minor bout of cursing in Portuguese.

"Oh bloody hell," said Pete to nobody in particular.

We unloaded some of the supplies and took stock of the water situation. We finally agreed that if everyone used water sparingly, we might slip by. Then we made introductions.

Will was a doctoral candidate from Oxford conducting studies on fish that emitted electric navigational fields. He was also studying an ornamental fish called the discus to determine if it could be sustainably culled for use in the international aquarium trade as a way for Caboclos to make money. Pete was Will's advisor at Oxford. He had been to the Amazon frequently, conducting studies of water chemistry and fish densities.

The floating house was dark inside and shaped like a rectangle with one bedroom at each corner, two bathrooms, and a kitchen. Two roughly made wooden tables and four wooden benches sat inside. Pete and Will sat in the two plastic chairs outside on the porch. The bedroms were empty, waiting for each of us to hang our hammocks there. Two shelves on a back wall held a set of solar-powered Delco Freedom car batteries that powered a forty-watt lightbulb, a shortwave radio, and a pump sunk below the house that forced water into a holding tank in the rafters. The tank fed the bathrooms, each equipped with a toilet bowl sitting above a hole in the floor and a shower head. The bathrooms came equipped with giant spiders and bats, extra amenities that provided interesting opportunities for wildlife observation. Waste water, including toilet flushing, simply flowed into the river beneath the house, which was, of course, where the pump feeding the showers was located. The kitchen had several shelves with supplies, and a two-burner propane stove. Green plastic mosquito netting sealed the rafters off from the living space below. This was not terribly effective. The door to the house had to stay open until dusk or everyone would literally bake under the tin roof like so many pies. At dusk, when the light was switched on, the door was closed, shutting off the breeze and theoretically keeping the mosquitoes and black flies, called *matukas*, out. It was a nice theory.

The only safe place from the *matukas* and the mosquitoes was under the mosquito netting of the hammocks. That night I laid in mine, a small candle lantern hanging over my head, reading a book. A howler shouted.

I smiled and stretched out in my suspended bed. The tonic of the jungle was working again. I slept soundly for the first time in days.

The mornings soon took on a routine. At about 5:30, just before sunrise, the troops of howlers would begin their low bellowing and slowly build until the small floating house seemed adrift in a wind. Sometimes the howlers would be close, nearly atop the house, other times farther away; but near or far, the entire forest echoed with their throaty yells.

I would lie in my hammock for a few minutes taking in the sound before walking out into the rest of the house for some morning coffee made cowboy-style, brewed with the grounds floating on top and served once they sank to the bottom. The breakfast menu usually consisted of a few crackers, a banana, maybe some instant juice. We sat outside on the front porch watching the morning mist rise through the trees across the river, enjoying the relative cool before the blasting heat we knew would come later. It was the only time, besides the daily afternoon rain, when the air cooled. The mosquitoes and *matukas* seemed to take time off during these few moments before the sun rose higher, perhaps saving a little energy for later assault waves.

A bat had taken roost above Pete's hammock. The varmint kept him awake late and woke him early, and each morning Pete would curse the bat.

"The little bastard!" he would seethe with his hair standing at odd angles and a bleary redness in his eyes, his fluorescent white legs sticking out from under a pair of shorts.

This amused Will, who seemed able to sleep soundly despite being in the same room. He would shuffle out of the bedroom, his long kahki shorts nearly falling off his hips. If his mother could have seen him, she would have immediately prepared a nice beef roast and Yorkshire pudding. Will had lost a fair amount of weight in the year he had been living in Tefé and in the floating house.

No wonder. The project hired Cabocolo women to cook. This may have been a good idea because it further integrated Caboclos into the project, making them part of the team, and it freed the researchers from domestic duties, giving them more time to work. But Caboclo women knew how to make one dish—*caldera*, a pot with rice and chopped fish. They just reached into the river and poured a few cups of brown water over the rice and fish and boiled until done. While that was quite efficient and certainly low on fats and cholesterol, it wore thin after a few days. The only addition was the omnipresent roasted manioc. This was poured on everything. Will ate huge quantities of it.

Immediately after breakfast Pete would light up a cigarillo and breathe in the forest air. Sometimes we watched the river dolphins swim by.

"Right" he would say with finality. "I think we should check the nets."

Will and Pete spent most of their days setting nets, checking them, collecting fish they had caught, and weighing and dissecting the animals. Pete took readings of the water's chemistry, the dissolved oxygen, the pH. If a fish was worth saving, they placed it in a jar of formaldehyde. They had, they said, discovered five new species of fish, a statement that amazed me.

"We would have expected that, actually," Will said. "There may be two thousand species in the basin, and only about half have been identified."

Nobody was even sure what many of the fish ate. A biologist had caught dozens of different fish, cut them open, and found seeds. She planted the seeds in tiny pots, and fifty different plants shot up.

"If you want to do biology," Pete said, "this is the place."

On the other hand, there were not many more dangerous places to do biology, either. One day Miriam and I returned to the house after a few hours under the canopy to find Will and Pete sitting at one of the tables inside. Pete was weighing some small catfish they had brought up in the nets. Will sat with his hand in the air taking notes.

"What's up with the hand, Will?" I asked.

"Something nicked me, I think. Not sure what it was. We were hauling up a net and taking the grasses from the floating meadow out of it when I felt fangs sinking into my thumb."

"A snake?"

"Maybe. Don't know, really. Could have been a spider, I suppose. I felt the bite and flung the thing off my hand and all I saw was a small black body flying away. Bloody hurts, though."

I looked at his thumb. It was swollen to about twice its normal size. Will's Caboclo assistant, Jonas, looked over my shoulder and mumbled with concern, which was no comfort to anybody. With so little known about the *várzea*, everyone relied heavily on the locals for the scoop on what was dangerous and what was not. If Jonas was worried, maybe Will should be worried, too.

Still, there was not much to be done. Will took an antibiotic and some aspirin. He did not know what the antibiotic and the aspirin would do, but he took them anyway. An hour later, near dusk, Pedro arrived to spend the night in the house. He looked at Will's thumb. His crew looked at Will's thumb. One of them hopped back aboard their boat and retrieved a small brown bottle.

"Here," Pedro said to Will, giving him the bottle. "The local people say this might work. I have no idea what it is." Will took a swallow.

"If he is still alive in the morning," Pete said with a laugh, "we'll know it worked."

Things like that happened all the time, Pete said. Why, a year ago he was bitten and barely made it out of the preserve alive.

"I went up like a bloody balloon," he recalled as he weighed his fish. "I looked like the Michelin man, so I evacuated to Tefé. Oh, the clinic was brilliant. I was getting delirious so they laid me out and strapped on an oxygen mask. I looked over at the oxygen tank. It said FOR INDUSTRIAL USE ONLY." He laughed.

"Just get me south," Miriam said. "I've told everybody, if anything happens to me, just get me out of here and to The South. They are not going to touch me in Tefé."

Some evenings, Will and Pete would eat the nightly *caldera*, retire to their room, and reemerge dressed head to toe. Each would pull on two longsleeved shirts taped at the wrists and two pairs of pants. Pete wore a floppy hat, Will a knit cap. Both wore headlamps. Though the sun was down, it was easily eighty degrees.

But they had to set a few nets to see what kinds of nocturnal fish they might catch. Unfortunately, the mosquitoes were more active at this time of evening. The layers of clothing were the only answer. Sweat dripped off their noses before they had even backed the boat out of the dock. They would return half an hour later, their clothes drenched, and shower in the river water that dribbled from the tank.

Usually, Pete would stroll out of the shower dressed in his finest evening wear: one in a series of shocking orange and blue Hawaiian shirts dotted with birds of paradise or hula girls or pineapples. We admired the shirts, and as he stood combing his blond hair over his bald spot and smoking his cigarillo, he looked for all the world like a tourist on Waikiki.

"Love the shirt, Pete," I said the first night he wore one.

"He always wears those down here," Will said in playful disgust.

"The reason I wear them here is my wife simply will not tolerate them at home."

"Good on your wife," Will said laughing.

"I think they are quite smart," Pete retorted, acting offended.

"All you need is a cold beer in your hand," I said.

"Oh, God, what I would do for a beer. It's bloody torture sitting around in this heat without beer."

At about seven, the time when Lafayette would turn on the short wave back at the project house in case anyone in the field needed to communicate, Miriam would fire up our radio for another confrontation. There was a lot to confront—the water, the shortage of gasoline for the outboards that Pedro had reported, the lack of any food variety. She liked jousting with Lafayette, and it always followed the same script.

"Tefé, Tefé. Tefé, Tefé." Silence. "Tefé, Tefé."

Lafayette broke in with the strange disassociated electronic voice that short wave lends to everything.

"Mamirauá, Mamirauá. Tefé."

"La-fay-etchay!" She shouted into the mike and everyone cackled with laughter.

I imagined Lafayette standing in his office, staring at the floor and scratching the back of his neck, wondering how he managed to land this job.

Meanwhile, Will worked on his notes, holding his left hand up in the air trying to keep the swelling down, writing with the right, murmuring "18.3 centimeters, 140 grams . . . anterior pectoral fin . . . caudal fin obliquely truncate . . . nuchal scutes fused across midline between occipital and dorsal. . . . "

Pete sat in his high-voltage shirt, writing numbers on water chemistry readings, smoking another cigarillo, a pair of headphones over his ears connected to a Walkman clipped to his waist, his thin hair falling over his eyes as his neck bobbed to the rhythm of Led Zeppelin. Somewhere in his head he jammed with Jimmy Page.

In the back bedroom the contingent of Caboclos played a loud game of dominoes.

"No, La-fay-etchay . . . " Miriam sighed.

"Been a long time since I rock and rolled!" sang Robert Plant.

"Nasal bone procumbent . . . " whispered Will.

The Caboclos slammed down some dominoes.

And the howlers in the trees greeted the night.

Pedro spent most of his time in the preserve living aboard the boat. He was a master's candidate in Portugal and was turning his studies on the effects of hunting on wild animal populations into a thesis. One day Miriam and I visited one of his work sites. We took an outboard up the Mamirauá and into a semicircular lake out of *Creature from the Black Lagoon.* The white riverboat had anchored in the still water. The lake was ringed on three sides with dense forest and floating meadows, huge islands of grass. The river flowed out on the fourth side, but the feeling was claustrophobic, eerie even. Forest sounds echoed in the quiet.

Hammocks were strung around the deck; a few Caboclos were eating crackers, sharpening machetes. Overhead, pairs of red and green and yellow macaws flew to some other perch in the forest. A kingfisher skimmed the surface of the water and nabbed a small fish in his beak. Green parakeets fluttered by. The howlers shouted at each other in the distance.

A young Caboclo paddled out of the forest toward the boat. Antonio climbed out of his canoe holding a handful of *camu-camu,* round, red fruits about the size of cannon shot. He gave some to me and to Miriam, who explained that *camu-camu* were rich in vitamin C and that someday the Caboclos might be able to grow them commercially. They were good, too, especially their slight bitterness, although after days of *caldera*, everything I put in my mouth that was not boiled fish and rice tasted wonderful.

We sat atop the boat and admired the amphitheater of beauty.

Every hour that went by in the forest seemed to unwind Miriam's tightness, a tightness I suspected had more to do with some past history than a sense of scientific professionalism. She smiled more freely, now, as she talked about her dolphin and manatee work, living in Florida, living in Tefé, living in the jungle. She hated Tefé, she said. She liked the jungle. Florida was okay. She had friends there. She liked the beach. Once, a cop stopped her coming from the beach because her Brazilian bikini was just a tad too Brazilian. She thought that was funny.

Miriam was thirty-four, attractive, smart. I wondered about the sacrifice involved in her work, living in the jungle away from the modern world. She had given up a lot to be here.

"Is it hard," I asked, "being thirty-four and single and living in a place like Tefé?"

"It can be. I got off the plane in Manaus from Miami with my computer and my books and my stuff and got on the boat at the port and started making the trip up here. I just laid in my hammock on deck with all my boxes around me and wondered what I was doing."

"Do you still wonder if it's worth it?"

"I have to do this for my country." She was, after all, Brazilian, though she sounded and acted so much like an American it was easy to forget she was born and raised in Pôrto Alegre, an industrial city in The South. "There are almost no marine biologists in Brazil," she said. "I had to go to the States to learn. I want to give something back to my country, like this project, and maybe teach someday."

I was sure that was all true. But I also thought that being in a place like this lagoon meant you could think about now and here and not about then and there, and all those fuzzy lines of life.

"Is it enough?" I asked.

She shrugged.

We sat in silence a moment and tried to spot more animals. She scanned the floating meadows for manatees. I looked at the back of my hand which had developed a tremendous red bump bigger than the dozens of other bites I could proudly display.

"Is it hard for you?" she asked.

I was surprised by the question.

"What do you mean?"

"You're my age. You've given up lots of things to be here, too."

I thought about my mood in Manaus, my depression in Tefé, the way thoughts had crowded in. I wondered if it had showed. I hoped not. I hate whining and hate feeling sorry for myself and certainly did not want it on display, especially for someone I admired, like Miriam.

"Don't you get tired of that?" she asked, referring to traveling.

"No," I answered. "I get to be here."

She smiled and knew what I meant. We knew each other better than we had thought. For us, here was incredible. Here was sensory overload. Here was exotic. Here there were macaws and caimans and monkeys and *camu-camu* and flooded forests.

Here was not there.

Pedro returned. He came paddling with two other canoes, each with two Caboclos. The Caboclos were shirtless. They wore shorts and rubber boots. Pedro was dressed in a long-sleeved work shirt, long pants, rubber boots, armor against the mosquitoes. All of them were drenched with sweat. They stepped up the ladder and into the riverboat and immediately gulped down big swallows of water. Then they took off their boots and poured the sweat out of them.

Pedro and his crew were cutting a cross-shaped trail through the jungle. Each arm of the cross would be two thousand meters long.

The trail would be used to take a census of animal life. In all, five trails would be cut in various parts of the forest in areas that saw hunting and ones that did not. The animal populations would be counted in each and guesses made as to what effect Caboclo hunting had on the densities.

"The people hunt only sporadically," Pedro explained in very careful English that sounded almost elegant. "This is because they have much fish, so hunting is almost like a sport for occasional food."

Howlers were their favorite target. When they could, they killed a Muscovy duck or even a curassow.

"Do they make *calderas* out of them?" I asked.

"Sometimes," Pedro said laughing. "Sometimes they cook them on a spit."

"Why are you working with machetes?" I asked, thinking that small chainsaws would be much more efficient.

"It is traditional," Pedro answered with a sigh and a shrug. "Besides, they do not know how to use power tools and it is a good way to get them involved in the project."

I figured that if Ayres' gamble was going to work, much of the credit would be this early employment of the Caboclos, though they had no idea exactly what the researchers were trying to do. Back at the floating house they often sat on the benches and stared at Will and Pete or Miriam and commented among themselves about the concern the scientists showed as they bent over tiny fish—fish you couldn't even eat—with their scalpels. Then they would snicker. Crazy gringos. They called the scientists *macaqueros*, monkey men, because Ayres first focused on the uakari.

After a break, everyone, including Miriam and I, got back into the canoes and paddled into the *várzea*. Anything that lived on the ground during the dry months now had to live in the trees. We floated past man-sized termite nests that had been built in the crotch of branches to escape the flood. Ants had moved into the limbs. They defended their woody homes fiercely.

Fish had learned to live on the small berries and fruits that fell in the water, a sound the Caboclos imitated to catch *tambaqui*. They baited hooks with berries and slapped at the water. It almost always worked.

When we arrived at the trail's end, where the crew had taken their break, they began slashing at overhanging branches and trunks to clear the path. The work was inhumane. Sweat poured out of their bodies. Biting ants and bark and mosquitos and wood chips stuck to their skin. Sometimes an ant colony fell into the canoes. This caused a brief flurry of panic until the nest could be tossed overboard.

But in general, everyone was blasé about danger. A Caboclo swung his machete just over me and a tarantula bounced at my feet. I looked at it for a moment, knowing that tarantulas are generally harmless.

"Hey, Miriam," I said, "see this spider? Think it's something to worry about?"

"Gee, I don't know," she answered as the spider walked to my boot. "I'll ask Joaquim."

She tapped the Caboclo in the bow of the canoe and asked him to have a look. He kneeled on the thwart and leaned over toward me.

"Aaiiee!" he screamed, whipping out his machete and thrashing at the spider, his eyes bugging out in terror until the spider was minced. He held the gooey carcass on the end of his machete and dumped it overboard.

Miriam looked back at me and smiled.

"Guess so," she said.

Will's finger became progressively worse. It was blue and swollen, though he insisted it did not hurt. Not much, anyway. The red bump on the back of my hand had developed a fascinating white crown. Pete walked out of the bedroom grumpier than usual.

"The bloody goddamn bat pissed on me all night, the little bugger."

Will and I laughed. Miriam laughed. Jonas and Antonio, who did not understand a word of English, laughed.

"Oh yes, quite funny," Pete said smiling. "Try sleeping with a bat pissing on you all night."

"Finger's worse this morning," Will said, showing Pete his bulbous thumb.

"Can't work with that," Pete told him, being a little fatherly.

"But we have a lot to do today sampling the floating meadows." I swallowed a sip of coffee and said, "Can I help?"

"Would you mind terribly?" asked Pete.

"Of course not. If all you need is labor hauling nets, I think I can handle that."

"That's all; even you could do it."

"Thanks, Pete."

"Oh, you might want to watch for the occasional anaconda, Brian," Pete said jokingly over his shoulder, referring to the giant water boas living in the *várzea*. They regularly grew to over twenty feet in length. The record was thirty-eight.

"And whatever laid into me," said Will, holding his hand in the air.

"Let's just hope we don't pull in any snakes, which we do one in five times," Pete replied, not kidding at all.

I dressed quickly and joined Pete and Will and Jonas in an outboard canoe. We sped up the Mamirauá to a smaller stream and motored to a grassy meadow floating in the current.

These floating meadows, islands of grass that thrived in the wet months, were an integral part of the *várzea* ecosystem. Manatees grazed on them, and small fish lived among them. Some species of spiders lived atop the grass. We pulled up to the island, a small one, and Pete and I got the net ready. Jonas sliced through the grass with his machete to carve out a section. Pete and I fed the net around the section and waited until the bottom weights had time to stretch the net vertically. Then he pulled on a line that closed off the bottom. We strained to pull in the grass and the net and whatever was inside. Once the net was aboard, we yanked up handfuls of grass, tossing them back in the water. Slowly, we uncovered a variety of life I never would have guessed would be living in the meadow. There were small catfish, water bugs, spiders, but, thankfully, no snakes. There was, however, an electric eel.

"Oh, God, do not touch the eel," Pete warned me.

Electric eels were common in the Amazon, and I had already seen several Will and Pete had brought back to the floating house. One was especially large, and even the Caboclos avoided it. The jolt from an adult eel could knock a man over.

We sampled three grassy islands and brought the buckets of fish back to the house where Pete and Will would sit and weigh and cut and describe, and amuse the Caboclos.

That night, when the door was closed at sunset and the mention of dinner floated in the conversation, I volunteered to cook. Leftovers from the night before and from lunch, a *caldera*, naturally, were available, but I was having a hard time looking forward to more boiled fish and rice; and besides, I was feeling a little useless and wanted to help.

"Sounds good, Brian," Pete said. "You cook, do you?"

"I make the best Spam carbonara you ever tasted," I said.

"You are joking," Will exclaimed, a little horrified.

"Of course," I lied. In fact, I was hoping there might be a can of Spam on the kitchen shelves. There wasn't. There was a can of what I think was corned beef, although I could not be sure since I could not read the Arabic script. The can, a product of Brazil's burgeoning beef industry, had been destined for the Middle Eastern deserts but had somehow escaped to Tefé instead. Finally, I spotted a two-day old *tambaqui* the Caboclos had caught. It sat, split in half, on the wood planks of the floor.

I picked it up and sniffed it, fully expecting to smell decay, but it had been salted. More rooting around on the shelves and the floor yielded a potato and an onion. I also found some pepper and corn oil. The cook, I thought, had been holding out on us.

I grabbed a machete off the wall, hacked the poor *tambaqui* into chunks, and heated some oil in the only skillet.

Jonas came into the kitchen and out the back door. Then he came back in the kitchen and stared at me, the skillet, and the oil.

As the oil heated, I sliced the potato and the onion, then tossed them into the skillet. The version of home fries spluttered and spit and filled the house with the smell of frying onion.

Jonas was joined by the woman who had been cooking our delicious *calderas*. She was not happy. I smiled. She stood with her mouth gaping open at the havoc I was wrecking in her kitchen.

I used the machete to scrape the potatoes and onions in the skillet as they browned.

"Smells very good, Brian," Pete shouted from the outer room.

I had attracted a crowd. The Caboclos stood in the doorway dumbfounded at the sight of frying potatoes. How would Martha Stewart handle this? "Yes, entertaining in the Amazon can be easy, and fun, too," I imagined her saying. "And now we will place the potatoes ever so decorously in the giant plastic bowl on the floor—presentation is everything, you know—and add more oil to the skillet to sauté our *tambaqui*. . . ."

I served the fried *tambaqui* and potatoes and onions. Pete and Will were grateful. There were tears of delight in their eyes because there was no *caldera* in their bellies.

"Oh, God, this is delicious," Pete panted between bites, demonstrating once and for all that a captive audience is the best audience.

I carried my plastic plate into the kitchen, where Jonas stood at the stove explaining to the gathered Caboclos, all of whom were eating *caldera*, what I had done to the *tambaqui*. I don't think they believed him. The cook sat on the wood planks just outside the back entrance and sloshed river water into the skillet. She gave me a dirty look. I offered the leftover fish and potatos to the Caboclos. They thought it was disgusting. The cook threw the food into the river. From this moment on, whenever they were near me, the Caboclos shook their heads and chuckled. The one Caboclo who had been sharing my room moved out.

Miriam, Antonio, and I set off early the next morning to check her receivers. Four of them had been established in the southern third of the preserve, three on tall tubular metal towers, and one at the top of a huge canopy tree. All were topped by square boxes containing a minicomputer and an antenna. The receivers, the first ever used in the Amazon to track aquatic mammals, collected electronic signals from tagged animals in order to chart their locations and swim patterns.

While some research had been done on the two species of dolphins, the *boto*, and the pink-and-gray *tucuxi*, such basic questions as whether or not they had "homes" and how far they swam and where they fed had gone unanswered. The Amazonian manatee was a mystery.

"It's a blank slate," Miriam said, as we chugged toward the first antenna, the one hidden up the giant tree. "Everything needs to be done, hormones, reproductive cycles, feeding, migration."

And the research was frustrating, mainly because she had yet to capture and tag a manatee. Manatees were incredibly secretive and shy, their grazing marks on the floating meadows being the only evidence of living animals Miriam had been able to see in months. She did have some manatee skulls. Though it was illegal, the shy mammals were hunted by Caboclos, who made a local delicacy of jellied manatee meat. But there was only one hunter left, a man named Clarindo, who could find a manatee on demand, and he had refused to help Miriam. He would not even allow her to look at skulls he had flayed, fearing they would fall into the hands of his ex-wife, a witch, who could then terrorize him by conjuring a *panema*, a deadly curse, on the skulls.

But Miriam had managed to capture dolphins and place transmitters on their fins. The dolphins were easy to find; we had seen half a dozen in the past few days, but they weighed up to two hundred kilograms, and hauling them aboard a dugout canoe to be tagged required herculean effort.

Antonio pulled the boat under the canopy and we rowed toward the tree. Short lengths of two-by-fours had been nailed into the trunk and Miriam used this stepladder to climb the eighty feet or so—the rest of it was underwater—to the tree's top. I followed. The view was magnificent. Light reflected off the water below, and for miles in all directions there was nothing but forest and rivers and lakes and flooded land. The brute size of it all was overwhelming.

Miriam used a laptop computer to download the telemetry and run a diagnostic check on the receiver. She always checked the receivers. They had failed just a few weeks after being installed, and Miriam suspected they might fail again. When they broke down the first time, the project contacted the Swedish firm that made them. The firm said it was impossible for them to fail. They had tracked deer in Sweden for years now and had never failed. The project was doing something wrong. The firm ran tests with rain and wind. The receivers did not fail. Finally, a technician in Sweden took a receiver into a sauna to imitate the Amazon. It failed. Changes were made.

The second receiver was in Antonio's village, Vila Alencar, near the banks of the Solimões. When we pulled up, a dozen laughing children ran to greet the boat. Things were hopping in Vila Alencar because Antonio, the son of the village "mayor," the patriarch, was going to kill his bull in a few days. A tall tree trunk had been turned into a pole and nailed from top to bottom with green bananas. When the bananas ripened, the bull was roast. The bull stood nearby, tied to a tree with a stringy rope. He spent a lot of time staring at the bananas.

Vila Alencar was a typical village for the preserve. All the families lived in shacks of one or two rooms furnished with hammocks and wooden and bamboo tables. The shacks sat on stilts about four feet off the ground, but almost every shack in the preserve had a brown line several feet above floor level where high water rose during very wet years.

Each village had its own manioc roasting shed. The manioc tuber was dug, cleaned, and soaked, then shredded into moist white bits. Then it was placed into a kind of giant wok over a three-foot-tall mud oven fueled with sticks. Most adult members of the community took turns constantly stirring the manioc until it was roasted into yellow crumbs.

Vila Alencar was also the site of the project's largest agricultural experiment. About half a dozen fruits found in the wild were being cultivated on long wooden tables under a green plastic net in the hopes that some might prove commercially viable. One, called graviola, was a green, spiky fruit that looked like a relative of the Malaysian durian. Despite the resemblance, it made a sweet, delicious juice.

Although Projecto Mamirauá had made progress, I had my doubts about the prospects for success. Would the Caboclos really postpone immediate paydays from logging or overfishing to preserve a better long-term future? Just as it had in el Petén, the idea of middle-class people with plane tickets out asking the desperately poor to reject a rope that could haul them up—even if only for a short time—seemed pretty cheeky.

Miriam suggested I attend a meeting in Vila São José. People from all over the preserved area would be there, she said, to discuss some issues that had arisen. I could just ask them what they thought.

Miriam and I left the floating house early that morning and motored down to Boca do Mamirauá.

Joaquim greeted us at Boca. Joaquim, the patriarch of the village, was an old smiling man about five feet tall with thick glasses, a permenant gray stubble on his cheeks, and a Marlboro World Championship cap on his head. The glasses were a recent addition. Joaquim had been seeing a local shaman about his increasing blindness until the project flew him to Manaus to see an ophthalmologist, who prescribed the glasses. He thought the glasses were nice but was amazed at how the shaman cured him.

Most Caboclos had been wary around me upon our first meetings, but Joaquim immediately shook my hand and slapped me on the back and said how nice it was to meet me.

Miriam told him who I was, why I was in the preserve. He was honored, he said, to know such an important man. I smiled and thanked him and wondered what Miriam had told Joaquim.

While most other villages had been set up on the small bits of dry ground to be found in the preserve, Boca was flooded. Wooden boards traversed the water to link one shack with another, and the few cattle in the village sloshed miserably through water past their knees. Joaquim's wife, Luzia, a wizened old indian woman, knelt on the floor of a floating shed preparing black round berries for fermentation into wine. Luzia knew more of the indian dialect than most other Caboclos, who spoke Portuguese, and recalled ancient ways that had passed from her parents. The scientists consulted with her often.

Miriam introduced me to Luzia, who said I looked like a nice young man. She asked how old I was. That was pretty old, she said, to not be married. But I looked younger. That was good. Maybe I could still find a wife. She wanted to know why I was not married. Miriam looked at me, waiting to see how I would answer.

"Because I have never found a woman like you," I told Luzia. She blushed and giggled, and the other, younger women laughed.

Joaquim and several others climbed aboard the *Ajuri*, the village's riverboat. We all set off into the confluence and chugged northwest into the Japurá, the two-cylinder diesel barely holding its own against the river. It was so slow, in fact, that whenever the boat passed a collection of huts, a canoe paddled out to meet the *Ajuri* and kept pace as more people climbed up the railing to join the cruise. The engine broke down twice. A half-hour outside Vila São José, Joaquim and several other men commandeered the aluminum outboard tied to the back and sped off, hoping to make the meeting on time.

But the *Ajuri* was not late at all. It did land at Vila São José about an hour later than planned, but none of the other people from villages around the preserve had been on time, either. The meeting still had not started.

Everyone gathered in the schoolhouse, a large open-sided wood structure with a tin roof. Old wooden desks had been arranged in a circle and all the men took seats. The women sat on a few wooden benches outside the circle. The leader of Vila São José, Alphonso, welcomed all the people to his village and asked them to introduce themselves, starting with Joaquim, who had changed into a longsleeved green shirt for the occasion. A young woman of about seventeen took notes. She was the schoolteacher, a girl who had managed to achieve the equivalent of an eighth-grade education, but one who could read and write and do arithmetic, which was more than almost any Caboclo could do. She lived in Boca but travelled from village to village teaching classes and relaying messages, like the one about this meeting, between communities.

Alphonso, a short, indian man, read a scripture quotation. Quoting scripture was something one did at official functions. It lent a weighty air to the proceedings.

The reading sparked a prolonged debate of its relevance to the condition of the Caboclos in the preserve, which, everyone seemed to agree, was improving slowly since the *macaqueros* had arrived. But there were problems. Some were still logging illegally, Alphonso said. The men turned to stare at a thin, dark man in a Rudiju Fantastic Sport Baseball T-shirt. He was rumored to be selling logs. His son was a project employee.

"The protected lakes should not be fished. Only designated lakes can be fished," Alphonso said.

"Yes, but your village is near good fishing," argued a man from another community. "What about my community? We have to fish."

There was jealousy among the villages. Vila São José, for example, had a solar panel nailed to the top of the schoolhouse, a gift from the project, that charged batteries used for powering lightbulbs. Other villages had no solar panels. And the project helped maintain the *Ajuri* for Boca while other communities did not even have an outboard. And the thirty or so isolated households in the *várzea*, those who did not live in a village, received none of the project's benefits and therefore figured the new system's rules did not apply to them.

As the men exchanged views, they unconsciously slapped their legs, demolishing the biting *matukas* and sending small drops of blood rolling down their skin.

Alphonso wound up the debate by asserting that the Caboclos had to stick together. "We must act as a community, not as individuals," he said. "We must stay together."

If they could not, how could they meet the threat from outsiders like the logger from Tefé who had come into the *várzea* waving guns and a piece of paper he claimed was a land title, even though there were no titles to the land? Even the Caboclos did not own land which was all held by the federal government.

"And what about the Manaus fishermen?" Joaquim asked. The only answer was the project, the *macaqueros*.

"We are privileged to live here," he said. "We can live in a preserve. It is up to us to keep it. We have to cooperate with the *macaqueros*."

After an hour the meeting broke for lunch. The women of the village brought out bowls of manioc and aluminum pots filled with *caldera* and arranged a buffet inside Alphonso's home. Everyone crowded into the house, helped themselves, ate, and then made room for another person. Alphonso handed me a plastic plate and dished heaps from each pot on it. He smiled, proud to show off the bounty of Vila São José.

The meeting did seem positive, and the Caboclos did seem to favor abiding by the project's rules. Later, on the trip back downriver, I asked Miriam if she thought their lives would improve.

She shrugged. "Maybe."

"You don't think so?"

"There are too many problems. Like cholera. It's endemic, now. They are at least a full day from the nearest doctor, maybe two by dugout. They just figure 'Well, so we lost one. There are so many. So what. Somebody died.' "

She told me a story about an old man in Tefé, a Caboclo, who had begged to use the radio at the project house to call into the *várzea*. His granddaughter had been ill, he pleaded, and he had not heard anything for a while. Miriam allowed him to use the radio. The granddaughter had died two days before.

"He just walked away," she said. "I asked him about it. He said, 'She had baby's disease.' 'Baby's disease?' I asked.

" 'Yes, baby's disease. Where the baby turns purple. There is nothing that can be done.' "

"The baby had been sick for a week and nobody brought her to Tefé," Miriam said, visibly angry at the man, who seemed not to care, at the country that made cars and jets and surfboards but could not put a doctor within reach of the Caboclos.

And then it hit me, something I had been trying to figure out for a long time, something that made me wonder in Taman Negara, disappointed me in Dominica, disturbed me in Petén.

It was funny, I thought, how gringos never talked about diarrhea when they talked and wrote about rain forests. White people from the northern hemisphere were always saying outrageous things about the jungles. In fact, gringos never called them jungles anymore. Kiss Tarzan of the Jungle, and darkest jungles, and steaming jungles, and savage jungles good-bye. The P.R. crescendo had turned the dangerous, exotic places I had dreamed of in my youth into rain forests, an innocuous name more Tolkein than Edgar Rice Burroughs. Rain forests were mystical places filled with wise native peoples who talked to nature and understood life. Rain forests were groovy.

But I stood by the rail of the boat and watched a young Cabo-clo woman nurse a small child as three others—all hers, all born before the woman was twenty—sat quietly at her feet, and wondered which of them would die from diarrhea. The Caboclos lived in the middle of the biggest rain forest on the planet, the vortex of eco-grooviness, and a lot of them shit themselves to death with cholera, dysentery, and parasites. If something was going to save the children from that, it would probably be medicine made in New Jersey by a stressed guy who drove a Lexus and never recycled. The First World had some answers of its own.

Nobody said anymore that tropical jungles are miserable places to live. They are glorious, yes, and vital to the planet, and maybe they really will produce miracle drugs.

But the irony dripped off the leaves like the raindrops that were now hurling themselves out of the sky. White women peeled off their shirts and let their breasts float in jungle streams trying to touch the essence of primitive. The Chocos, meanwhile, thought bras were a pretty hot invention, and Keladong bin Bulat had fallen in love with home-delivered meals, and the kids on Dominica stuttered reggae-gangsta rap. Whenever they had contacted some of the miracles of the developed world, they wanted them; for good or evil, they wanted them, soaked them up like sponges. How presumptuous of us to take off our clothes and tell them to stay put in the jungles. They wanted to be more like us while we were trying to be more like them. They had all the answers they needed from the rain forest, thank you very much. Please pass the remote control.

The air was cooler my last night in Mamirauá, the night Miriam and I left the floating house to retrieve Pedro from his boat in the forest. The last sun was turning the line of trees on one side of the river a deep orange. The trees on the other side were in shadow.

We stopped by a huge floating meadow and quietly paddled through it while Miriam looked for signs of manatee feeding. They were there. They were fresh, and Miriam knew there was no chance of seeing the manatees that made them. Not on this day. Manatees were rarely surprised. But we did see a three-toed sloth lounging in a treetop.

We motored out of the meadow and let the boat drift in the current.

"Listen," she said.

From somewhere, maybe a few yards away, we heard the sounds of deep breathing. I looked at Miriam, who smiled a broad smile.

"My dolphins."

A few moments later, there was more breathing. Two gray dolphins surfaced in front of the boat, and Miriam smiled again.

We had seen dolphins before. Several times, while we were simply sitting on the front porch of the house, the pink-and-gray animals would arch their backs out of the water, take a breath, and submerge into the milky river. But here, it felt as though the dolphins, just a few feet away, were swimming with us. They were not. It was just a lucky accident.

"Listen," she said again.

The dolphins resurfaced and breathed.

"Did you hear that? One of them has a cold. Listen to it wheeze."

When the dolphins returned to the surface, I could hear the congestion through one of their blowholes. I laughed out loud.

Miriam smiled. We felt good. Here was a pretty great place indeed.

It was dusk by the time we reached Pedro. A full moon had risen. He climbed aboard and took the tiller and motored through the night. Overhead one star after another popped out from behind the sky's black curtain to take a bow, and, in the water, the small stars of caiman eyes peered at us from the forest's edge. The moonlight reflected off the river. Pedro shut off the engine and we drifted, saying nothing.

I realized suddenly why jungles always made me feel so good. Why the tonic worked. Why I had spent so much time looking for something in them. It was the impossible luck of it all. There was no ultimate design, no meaning, no wisdom written in the trees. This forest, this scene, this moment was just a zany roll of the cosmic dice as if the Gothic builders had heaved the stone blocks and flying buttresses and gold leaf into the air and it had all come down as Chartres. In fact, if there were a God, He would spend His tough days visiting the man-made cathedrals and mosques and temples, where people believed in Him and asked favors and prayed for victories over the other guys who called Him by other names. And then He would come here into this green cathedral. He would crack open a beer, walk around in His boxers, put His hands on His hips and mutter, "How about that?" at the miracle of all this being thrown together out of the dust of the Big Bang. He would shake his head at the wild stroke of luck.

Meanwhile, people disillusioned with the world they had made in other places came and knelt and prayed in the green cathedrals, supplicants seeking a momentary respite from complexity, an end to the grayness where life and meaning are undefined. But all the jungles could offer were moments, glimpses.

The green cathedrals were accidents and even more precious for that, but that was their only lesson. Accidents happen. Sometimes they could be good. Now, for crying out loud put your clothes back on and go home. Get on with life.

It took the Amazon to finally make me see it. Miriam saw it, too.

She was stealing moments here, moments like those I had been stealing when life seems in sharp focus through nature's lens; but, in the end, she knew the dilemmas were still there—the diarrhea, the poverty, the social progress—and the green cathedrals were coming down. The jungles were going, and a handful of scientists and $4.3 million were not going to stop it. Still, if the universe had gambled and come up with the *várzea*, well, you never knew, did ya?

Two dolphins surfaced and breathed and dipped under the water. I looked at Miriam, who was smiling.

"Is this enough?" I whispered.

"Yeah," she answered. "This is enough."

I left the *várzea* the next day. I woke early with the howlers and padded into the common room. Pete was there, sitting at the table looking like a beat-up prize fighter. He had become a uakari. His face was red, and he, like all of us, was covered in bites. He looked at me and murmured, "Goddamn bat!"

He had tried a sheet of plastic over his mosquito netting, which made the hammock hot and stuffy, but even then, the bat dribbled piss onto the plastic like Chinese water torture. Pete, of course, could have avoided all of it. He could have stayed in England and so could Will. Will could have studied Scottish salmon for his doctorate and Pete could have taught and consulted and never been bitten or pissed on or gotten sunburned. Life would sure have been more comfortable.

But Pete craved the exotic, too. As he and I stood over the river at the edge of the front porch brushing our teeth, we looked across the water where the mist was rising in the trees. Pete spit a mouthful of toothpaste into the water and stood motionless for a moment just staring.

"This is a bloody goddamn beautiful forest, isn't it, Brian?" he said.

I took a hot shower once I reached the project house back in Tefé and decided to work on the bump on the back of my hand, the one that was now oozing pus. I squeezed a little, then opened it. A tiny white maggot wriggled out.

I packed up the following morning and thanked Lafayette for all of his help. He had to run, he said. There was a crisis of some sort. He was sorry. He grabbed his brown leather fedora and his English Lavender bag and scurried through the front gate by the pool and off into the heat.

I went downstairs and picked up some notes I had left on a desk. Suddenly Will burst through the door.

"What are you doing here?" I asked. "You're still supposed to be in the forest." Then I noticed that Will looked as though he had died several days before. He was extremely pale and clammy and seemed barely able to stand.

"My thumb," he said. "About sundown last night, I was unable to pass water. My body swelled and I had a sudden fever. At about ten, we got in the outboard and Jonas and I started back to Tefé in the dark. Then the sky opened up and we had buckets of rain. God, it was awful. Jonas helped me reach the clinic in town, but they had no idea what do so they just pumped me full of antibiotics. It seemed to help. I'm much better today."

Miriam peeked through the door. Carlos was waiting outside. It was time for me to leave. I did not want to go. I was leaving something behind, here, in this place where nobody goes, something I had carried around a long time. I was worried I would miss it.

"So long, Brian," Will said shaking my hand. "If you ever get back to Oxford, call me and we will terrorize the women together. If this place doesn't do me in first."

Miriam walked out the gate with me. Carlos kicked open the passenger door. Miriam gave me a hug and a smile that said "maybe in another life." I climbed into the car and as Carlos pulled away, I waved good-bye.

"So how about the Brazilian soccer team?" Carlos asked in Portuguese, whacking me on the knee.

I smiled. Carlos grinned his gummy grin and we bounced down the road toward a gray horizon.

q 5/06

326